COMPETE
EVERY
DAY

Compete
Every Dy!

- John

**THE NOT-SO-SECRET SECRET TO
WINNING IN YOUR WORK AND LIFE**

COMPETE EVERY DAY

JAKE THOMPSON

Clovercroft Publishing

Compete Every Day

©2020 by Jake Thompson

Published by Clovercroft Publishing, Franklin, Tennessee

Edited by Lee Titus Elliott

Cover Design by Jake Thompson

Interior Design by Adept Content Solutions

Printed in the United States of America

978-1-950892-52-5

To my wife Elena, whose uncondi-
tional love, support, and encouragement
allowed me to pursue my dreams.

To my parents Steve and Sandra for always
believing in and encouraging me to dream big-
ger, do more, and leave a positive legacy.

To my friends Adam and Ty for making sure
I pursued this "compete every day" dream.

To my mentors: Carrie, Chris, Grant, Michael,
and Amy; thank you for believing in me,
encouraging me, and helping me to elevate
my work in order to elevate my impact.

To every single person who has bought
something, shared something, or supported
something we've created since our humble begin-
nings in the trunk of my car, circa 2011.

Hey, it's Jake here...
I'm the book's author.

I hope you receive incredible value from this book. I wanted to give you three ways you can continue building your Competitor Mindset after finishing this book:

Listen to the Compete Every Day podcast. My weekly show features guests sharing stories, lessons, and resources to help you continue building your leadership skills, mindset, and life. Available on iTunes, Spotify, and Google Play or at Podcast. CompeteEveryDay.com!

Order motivational apparel and gear. Use the code BOOKCLUB to get 15 percent off your next order at CompeteEveryDay.com.

Empower your company & team to Compete Every Day. I speak all over the world to organizations, athletic programs, and schools about how to integrate the Competitor Mindset into team culture to improve grit, productivity, & success. Learn more at Speak.CompeteEveryDay.com

A special invitation to join the Compete Every Day community.

You are invited to join the thousands of ambitious Competitors claiming victory in their professional and personal lives in our free Facebook community at:

www.Facebook.com/groups/CompeteEveryDay

Inside this community, you will find thousands of driven leaders just like you who are making strong choices to compete every day in their work, workouts, and life.

I am excited to meet you, encourage you, and hold you accountable to achieving the important goals you've set for your career and life.

Contents

01

Success in Life and Sports

What's true in sports is true in life

Deep down, I believe we all want to hoist a championship trophy.

There's a yearning within us to win *something*—a sports championship, a promotion at work, the heart of someone we are destined to love as "the one," or a local fitness competition. We want to be a winner capable of achieving success.

Think about it: How emotionally driven do we get when our favorite sports team wins? Fans celebrate more than the athletes who put in the years of work for that title. They feel invested in the championship, despite having never played one snap on the field. And they will always believe that they own some small piece of this title.

We never forget where we were watching when *our* team won *our* first championship.

As fans, we believe it's *our trophy, too.*

We do the same in the political arena. Election day every four years is a joyous or heartbreaking event on the basis of whether *your* party won or lost. We feel ownership in the process and ride

1

the emotional high or low of the outcome, even though we are just 1 in 138 million votes.

It's an innate human need to be a winner—because winners *belong.*

Our ancestral history dates back to the time of the cave dwellers, when survival depended on the tribe. We needed to belong to a community in order to survive the dangers of the world. The better equipped you were to provide, the higher your status in the community—and the safer you were within the community, because no members of the community would ostracize their best providers.

We aren't hunting wild game on the plains anymore, but our mentality hasn't changed much. We still see winners as the most valuable people in society. Sports winners are paid handsomely for their on-field performances. Hollywood's winners pack the box office and adorn the covers of magazines. Even your local small Texas town identifies its winners by who sits on the school board or city council and by who wears the letter jackets on Friday nights.

Winners are the ones who reap the rewards in life. If you hold the trophy, you hold the power and the status of achievement.

Many believe that life is *easier* for winners and that because of who they are, they don't have to struggle. Goals are handed to them. Roadblocks are opened up. We know that like sports, life has winners and losers. And if we get to be ones among the winners, then goals become easier to achieve, friends easier to make, and bank accounts easier to fill.

The only way to make life exponentially better is to be the winner—because, if not, then we'd have to be the loser, right? At least that's what social media leads us to believe.

As kids, we believed we were going to be winners. We started to learn, as we grew older, that not everyone was going to be a winner. The simple fact of competition is that you need a loser in order to have a winner.

I had an (almost unrealistic) belief while growing up that I was going to be a winner in life. I assumed that because I had the right attitude, a decent work ethic, and good connections, win-ning—and everything I assumed came with it (money, status, attention from the opposite sex)—was just a given.

What a pile of crap that was.

Flash forward some years later; instead of being a "winner," I found myself in a hole. I drank daily, changed girlfriends more often than I changed socks, and watched my bank account shrink as I outspent what I had made. I quit what I thought was my dream career and struggled to find any purpose in work I was doing. Yet I still believed that things would improve and that I'd be winning one day—I just needed to find the magic "tipping point" that would change everything.

Do you know that feeling? You look frantically for that one book or podcast or YouTube video or relationship that will change your entire life overnight. I believed if I could just find "it," I'd go from struggling to succeeding in the snap of finger. That "one thing" would change everything.

Can you relate?

Have you ever tricked yourself into believing that if you just:

- Found "the one," you would feel complete.

- Started this new diet, you'd finally be in a shape that makes you happy.

- Read this one specific book, you'd solve all of your business problems overnight.

The one thing about that list above is that when you read it—the one line you've told yourself probably stands out as believ-able, but the others? They sound ridiculous. Our excuses always sound sweet to our own ears, but to everyone else?

They sound like crap.

I was swimming in my own lies about success until I finally remembered the one truth I'd known earlier in my life but had forgotten.

I'd forgotten sports.

The beauty of sports is its meritocracy: the best player or team wins. Period. You can't talk your way into a league championship. You can't buy an MVP. You have to *earn* your successes on the field, one play at a time, every game and every season.

But the real way you earn your success on the field is by committing to the work off of it, throughout every day in the off-season and every practice rep.

"You earn your championships in practice—you just pick them up on game day."

Somewhere along the way, I made the mistake of believing life worked differently. I had believed that to be a winner in life, it came down to what you looked like, whom you knew, and what lucky breaks you fell into. I had made the mistake of spending my youth obsessed with being liked, with being in shape, and with waiting for a lucky break rather than following the same path I had followed in sports to be able to play quarterback for my hometown team.

I had forgotten that sports mirror life. I started to realize that what I'd been missing I'd known all along.

Success is earned every day. Some are born with more talent or given more opportunities, but to win, you still have to do the work before games and then to seize the moment when the chance for success comes. If I wanted to be a winner in life, it came down to what I was doing to "earn championships in practice" every day. This "aha" moment changed everything. I started obsessing over competition and winning over competitors.

- What made winners so successful?

- What did they do to get to where they are now?

- And, most important, what did they do that I can replicate to be successful in my life?

I began researching successful leaders in sports and life to answer these questions. I watched games, studied teams, and made notes. I experimented with my work and life.

I discovered that being a winner—in sports and in life—doesn't require a very complicated formula. You don't need to have a PhD or be able to pat your head while rubbing your stomach. Winners aren't hiding some magic potion from you. And to be honest, it isn't one big "thing" that makes a winner.

It is, actually, a lot of very small things—mundane and seemingly unimportant choices that, when compounded, one on top of the other, create massive growth.

It's not a single interaction, extra sale, or special person that is going to create the incredible life-changing moment that transforms us forever into winners.

It's the simple, small choices every day.

Hold on; if it's just simple, small choices that make the biggest impacts, why doesn't everyone make those choices? It can't be that easy, because everyone isn't winning.

Just because something is simple doesn't necessarily make it easy. However, with the right mindset—*a Competitor's Mindset*—simple can become *easier* than most people realize.

This book is designed to help you identify the key choices you can make to win in the key areas of your life (career, fitness, relationships) so that you can begin to discover how much *more* potential is within you.

Each chapter will identify and detail a specific action trait that successful Competitors share. You'll learn how these traits are not the result of natural abilities but key choices made on a daily basis.

To help you digest and apply each trait, I've included two key sections at the end of each chapter, "How To" and "Chapter Takeaways." "How To" will provide a list of ways you can immediately incorporate this trait into your professional and personal life, broken down by each area. "Chapter Takeaways" will summarize three-to-six key lessons from the chapter so that you can continue to reinforce your own Competitor Mindset.

I believe in your ability to win. Turn the page so we can start identifying—and making—the choices to help you do just that.

02

Why Competition Matters

We were desperate and running out of time.

There's less than a minute left!

Kyle, go. You can do it.

No, I'm done. Jake, just give it a shot.

Wait; how much is it? Can I do that?

I don't know, Jake; just go…pick it up! Hurry!

I struggled for a good twenty-five seconds to lift that barbell off the ground, but I somehow lifted it all the way up to my hip for a completed rep. I had no idea how much weight it was, just that it was heavy.

Holy smokes, Jake. That was 455.

Wait, what? I had lifted forty-five pounds more than my previous best.

I had never come close to that before. I had maxed out at our gym just a week earlier at 405. That was a big deal for me to finally break 400 pounds on a dead lift movement that I had struggled with. Yet in the middle of a competition, with the clock running out and my teammates yelling at me, I blew that previous best away.

How?

Our bodies are capable of so much more than we give them credit for. Our heads tell us to slow down, because we can't keep running at that fast pace. Our brains yell that we can't keep going or "we'll die."

Our brain doesn't know how to respond when we push ourselves into a state of discomfort by going harder or farther or longer than we had previously. Our ancestors ran as hard and as fast as they could while hunting wild game and surviving a bear attack. That "fight-or-flight" thought process still remains deeply embedded in our brains. So when you start feeling uncomfortable during a workout or a run and your brain doesn't identify any life-or-death threats, it's going to encourage you to slow down. "Why be uncomfortable when there's no life-threatening reason to be?"

Through Discomfort Comes Growth

Discomfort sets in when we experience something we've never felt before. We move outside of our comfort zone and into the unknown—and our body responds as if it's threatened. Success lies in our ability to mentally manage the discomfort and still lean into it. It's in our ability to view discomfort as a *growth opportunity*, instead of a threat.

It's pushing ourselves to be uncomfortable during a workout that increases our physical and mental strength and endurance.

It's having that uncomfortable conversation that helps us address relationship issues and thrive.

It's stepping into uncomfortable, new situations, like job interviews, that provide us the space to pursue our dream career.

Achievements of value in this life will require you to lean into discomfort for the sake of something better. A flower doesn't gently grow and bloom from a seed. It has to fight and to force its way through the soil and rock to the surface, where it can continue to grow in the sunlight.

You're going to have a weird feeling in your stomach. You're going to question whether or not you have what it takes. But you have to continually remind yourself that what you're doing and who you are becoming by leaning into the discomfort are more important than temporary feelings you have in the moment.

Growth is an uncomfortable process, because it's only by stepping out of what we know and what's comfortable that we're able to push ourselves to stretch into someone capable of more.

Enter Competition

Jeremy Jamieson, together with two of his colleagues at the University of Rochester, published a research study[1] reviewing how our brains respond to stresses while evaluating situations we encounter as *challenges*, as opposed to how we respond to *threats*. When we perceive something as a threat, our bodies go into survival mode. Fear and anxiety increase, causing our heart rate and blood pressure to shoot upwards.

Our body's natural "fight-or-flight" response is designed to let us spring into action. But with most of the *perceived threats* we encounter today, we aren't actually in physical danger—it's just our mind perceiving threats to our status, belonging, or relationship.

That response floods our body with excess levels of stress hormones that leave us anxious without an outlet when our brain realizes there's no *actual* physical threat. Our brain, in essence, overestimated its response to a threat that isn't as dangerous as it had initially believed.

On the other hand, research shows that your body responds to a *challenge* by priming you to rise to the moment. Testosterone increases, adrenaline rushes through you, and your body is activated to *go*, improving your performance in that moment. Unlike the moment when you're battling anxiety from a false physical threat, the increase of testosterone reduces the social anxiety you feel so you can focus more clearly on the challenge at hand.

Our bodies combat threats by increasing stress and social anxiety and by creating a feeling of being anxious to the point where we respond to challenges by increasing our focus, decreasing our anxiety, and priming ourselves for performance. The difference simply comes down to what you've trained your brain to see: a threat to run from or a challenge to rise up to.

And what more is competition than a challenge to meet? Our bodies are primed to take on a competitive *challenge*.

In the case of my workout, my body was pumped with adrenaline, because that situation set up a perfect opportunity to outperform my perceived "limit."

- I had a rapidly approaching deadline (thirty seconds left).

- There was no threat if I failed—we already had a baseline score—so this was pure challenge.

- I was oblivious to the weight—I had no idea how much weight was on the bar, so my brain was prevented from talking me out of it.

By placing myself into this competitive atmosphere, I created an opportunity to find out what I was truly capable of. My brain and body are primed to perform when a challenge is issued. By intentionally viewing life through the lens of competition, we can train our brains to respond accordingly, to rise to a challenge instead of responding to a threat.

Friendly Competition

A friend of mine is a college football coach. One day, while he was giving me a tour of campus and his team's facilities, we got into the subject of competition. The coach shared that he gets four leaders together and then has them "draft" their teammates for off-season workouts. Each team will then compete against each other to earn points in the classroom, in the weight room, in practice drills, and in film sessions.

Make all of your classes and tutoring sessions this week? Points for your team.

Forget your playbook before a meeting? Your team loses points.

You get the idea: every activity is designed around earning or losing points to force the players to step up their games. Instead of being accountable to the coaches, each player is accountable to his teammates and captain, because no one wants to be on the last-place team each week. It's a matter of pride.

The coach loves this drill, because it creates an environment of friendly competition, in which the players are accountable to each other and are forced to give strong efforts in both football and school.

"We need competition," he told me. "It's in our blood to face against something or fight for something, to push ourselves to want to be better, and there's nothing like a challenge (from your teammates or the world) to push you past what you think you're capable of and to a whole new level. That new level is exactly we need from our players to be successful."

This coach created a game to help bring out the best in his players. He pitted them against each other, not with a position on the line but with their pride, and he used it to help them raise their game in school and sport.

Competition forces us to face challenges that create the crucial moments when we can finally discover how much more we have within us than we ever thought possible.

Aretas / ar'-e-tas /

Arete is the Greek word for excellence. You'll commonly see it referred to "excellence" by businesses in the marketplace.

But as authors Po Bronson and Ashley Merryman point out in their book *Top Dog: The Science of Winning and Losing*[2], excellence sells the definition of *arete* short. The authors changed the word to *aretas* for the purposes of their book and to illustrate its (more) important true meaning:

> *Aretas* is not just excellence—but it is the *revelation* of excellence, notably through competition.

Aretas is the process through which excellence is *revealed*.

Instead of what you believe you're capable of, competition reveals your true ability—and how much greater it always is than you give yourself credit for.

But we can't discover how much more we have within us unless we're willing to step into the arena of competition. This is true for sports, and it's true for life.

Many people live their entire lives submitting to those voices in the backs of their heads that whisper:

- *"You aren't the right person to do that."*
- *"You'll never be as successful as _____ is."*
- *"You can't."*

Those whispers cut like tiny blades and leave small scars behind that we accept as marks we can't escape. We believe the whispers are true and tell us who we are—while simultaneously reminding us of who we'll "never" be.

We don't dare leave our comfort zones when we submit to the whispers. We think they keep us safe and protected from what's out *there* in the unknown. We are tricked into believing we're better by listening to the voices and by settling for those limits.

We're tricked into sacrificing our potential and leaving "money" on the table of life.

Tied to a Rope

Most of us grow up being told what we can or can't do.

The more we hear something—and the more we *tell ourselves* something—the more we believe it, regardless if it's true or not. Words take hold like roots into the foundation of our lives, influencing every choice we make. We evaluate our identities through the lens of that influence, and it either helps or hurts which choices we make to align with those identities.

I went to the circus a number of times while growing up. I was always fascinated by the massive elephants, but part of me feared they would turn and start running toward the crowd. You have these enormous animals, yet they're so docile and safe within the confines of the circus arena.

I later learned why.

When the circus receives a baby elephant, it ties a strong rope around the young elephant's neck and attaches that rope to a secure pole. Try as it may, the baby elephant cannot walk past where the rope will let it. It's not strong enough to pull the pole out. Eventually, after wrestling with the rope multiple times, the elephant gives up pulling on the rope and decides to stay where it is.

The trainers take the elephant back to the rope and pole after every show and place the rope around its neck. The cycle repeats—the elephant pulls on the rope, trying to break away, and, after much struggle, it gives up, to settle down where it is.

As the elephant grows older (and much, much larger), it still believes the rope is its leash. As an adult, the elephant is more than capable of ripping the pole from the ground or tearing the rope, but it remembers only its struggles as a baby and chooses to accept the rope's limitations.

A 13,000-pound animal is held in place by a small rope around its neck—not because of the strength of the rope but because of the strength of the elephant's limiting beliefs.

Our beliefs can build our freedom or our prison.

This is also what happens when we accept those whispers and self-limiting beliefs as facts. Instead of discovering what we each can *actually* do in our career, in our health, or in our life, we each tie ourselves to a tiny stick in the ground and live our entire life as a shell of what we each could be. Our power goes dormant without ever having the opportunity to reveal itself.

In her blog *The Top Five Regrets of the Dying: A Life Transported by the Dearly Departing*, author Bronnie Ware documents her experiences working in hospice. She interviewed people about life, and, at the end of their lives, what was the biggest regret they carried? The number-one regret?

I wish I'd had the courage to live a life true to myself, not the life others expected of me.[3]

These people had gotten to the end of their lives, unable to change the choices they'd made and the limitations they'd accepted as truths. Like the elephants in the circus, they were born with great power and potential but had allowed the rope of what others had said and believed to limit them. They walked around as adults, carrying ropes from which they were more than capable of breaking free but believing they couldn't.

Your conscious and unconscious beliefs influence every decision you make. Do you believe yourself to be a courageous person? Then you'll behave that way in a social setting by approaching a stranger to say "Hi" and initiate a conversation. Do you believe yourself to be a "bad" public speaker? If so, then you'll avoid any opportunity to speak in front of people, as if public speaking is the bubonic plague.

Our actions are reinforced by our limiting or limitless beliefs. The good news is that, unlike that elephant who lives forever limited by the rope around its neck, we have the ability to change our beliefs and the way our brains respond to situations.

You have the opportunity to burn away your limiting beliefs and replace each belief with a Competitor's perspective, capable of running with power and freedom toward your best life.

I don't know about you, but I'd rather live like an elephant on the African plains, roaming wild, free, and full of power, than one chained to an imaginary anchor in the ground.

Every Day Is a Competition

I *love* competition.

I was always a smaller athlete while growing up. No matter what sport I played. there were bigger, stronger, faster, and more talented players on my team. I could lift weights and run all day, but I was never going to be the most athletic player on my team.

I embraced competition because it was my opportunity to prove I could *outwork* and *outsmart* more talented players. I didn't care if they had more God-given talent. I believed I had more inner fire and determination to beat them. It didn't matter what they did; I wanted to do it *better.*

Pickup basketball. Off-season football drills. Video games. My attitude was that even if other players had more natural ability, I was determined to die on the field before acknowledging defeat.

I carried this same competitive mindset throughout every other area of my life after I finished playing team sports. I craved the rush of adrenaline competition gave me—and, even more than that, the rush that came with winning those competitions.

School projects. Dating the "cool" girls. Off-season workouts.

My entire life became a competition with everyone else. I believed my self-worth was validated by winning these imaginary competitions. My identity was tied up in competing against other people, and my worth was based on how the competition went.

If I won, I had a chance to be popular and liked in school. If I lost, I might be cast out to the "uncool" crowd. In my immature and limited perspective, this was the equivalent of heaven or hell, life or death. I craved being liked and accepted, so competition became the route through which I could claim both.

Or so I believed.

Here's the craziest part of my mindset: *I had zero control over all those I went up against.* I didn't control their talents, where they came from, whom they knew, what they were focused on, or how hard they were working for their goals.

I didn't even control whether they even realized I was competing against them! Of them all, 99.9 percent of were oblivious that some obsessively competitive guy was trying to beat them in a race they didn't even care about.

I was investing all of my time, all of my energy, and all of my emotions into competing against all others, and *I didn't control them.* We have control of only three things in life: our effort, our attitude, and our emotions, and I was giving total control of those things to competitors I didn't control.

This type of mindset isn't sustainable, as you can imagine. You eventually run out of steam, because comparison is a never-ending rat race.

Think of an Olympic sprinter.
She lines up at the starting gates, feet secure in the blocks and body poised to explode forward when the gun sounds.
Bang!
She fires out, sprinting with every ounce of energy toward a finish line 100 meters directly ahead. But, for some reason, she starts to think:
What's everyone else doing?
I wonder where everyone else is?
She turns her head to her left and then back to her right, trying to get a glimpse of where the other racers are. She then twists her shoulders and neck to look behind her. And do you know what happens to her?
She slows down, she runs out of her lane, or, just maybe, she trips and falls down.
Our bodies are not designed to run at their peak speed in one direction if our shoulders are twisted, if our heads are turned, and if we're doing anything but pressing forward in that one direction with everything we've got.
You reach your true top-end speed only by focusing on your finish line, by staying in your lane, and by pushing ahead with everything you've got toward your finish line. This is true in sports.
And this is true in life.
My competition isn't with you. It isn't with anyone reading this book and, for that matter, with anyone who isn't reading this book. My greatest competition is with myself.
It's with that person I see in the mirror every morning when I wake up and again every night before I go to bed.
The person I crave to outwrite, to outsell, and to outwork? Myself.
Just like that Olympic sprinter, if I want to reach my true potential—my top gear in life—I need to quit wasting my time, my energy, and my efforts worrying what all others are doing in their lanes and instead focusing only on my own lane.
I needed to compete with myself, and I needed to find a way to beat my yesterday, every day.

My entire life changed the moment I realized this.
I'd spent years investing the things I control (time, effort, energy) into worrying about things outside of my control (everyone else). I was emotionally spent and mentally exhausted. I suddenly felt rejuvenated with this new focus on myself and my own race.

I discovered that comparison with and competition against others weren't permanently sustainable but that competing against yourself was. In fact, the challenge of going up against yourself constantly renewed you!

My strongest competition occurs with who I was yesterday, and, just the same, your strongest competition occurs with *who you were before* you picked up this book.

There are two mistakes that most people make every day.

The first mistake is believing that you can float passively through life and still succeed without competing. It's this crazy idea that if you "believe" success will come your way, it will magically manifest itself in areas of your life. You don't have to take action. You don't have to take on any challenges. You simply imagine your success, and then it happens.

That is crap.

Sitting passively and waiting on things to happen for you is *choosing* to intentionally put yourself out of position to seize an opportunity when it comes. You don't wish for success—you compete for it. You *choose* to take action every day. You intentionally *choose* to step into the arena of life's competition.

The other mistake happens when we invest our lives trying to compete against all others and when we constantly measure our worth against where we sit in comparison to all others' successes and failures.

We don't control those other people. We don't know what head start they had, what connections they've made, or what talent they were born with. Yet we waste all of our limited resources trying to keep up with them—instead of using those resources to improve ourselves.

The problem with comparison is that there's always someone doing better than we are and that there's always someone doing worse than we are. We'll never experience enough joy when comparing our wins to those ahead of us, and we'll burn ourselves out trying to keep up with them. Instead of celebrating the progress we've made, we're miserable, because we still aren't to the level of _____. (I'm sure you can drop someone's name in there).

Instead of passively "believing" in success, until it (never) happens or instead of investing in a pointless competition against others, we need to choose to compete against ourselves and the things in our life that continue to prevent us from reaching our true potential.

Things that appear on the outside, like....

- Big risks
- Lack of experience
- Bad bosses
- Snooze alarms
- Crazy exes

But if we peel back the layer, we discover that what we need to take on are

- Our fears
- Our doubts
- Our self-limiting beliefs
- Our bad habits we've allowed ourselves to build
- Our toxic relationships that we continue to nurture instead of ending

These are the things we're competing against, because these are what stand between us and our true potential every day. And if you're like me, every day you're butting up against friction from these forces.

You feel great some mornings. Your wake up *energized* just before your alarm even sounds and continue to roll throughout the day energized, completing task after task for your professional and personal goals.

And then the other mornings, you hit snooze repeatedly. Again. And again. Maybe even a third time for good measure. Your temptations for junk food at lunch or for that extra drink at happy hour are unstoppable. You talk yourself into believing that "it's okay" if today is wasted because you've got tomorrow. It's as if you've resigned yourself to losing the day's competition before it ever begins.

Some days you have "it," and some days you don't. At least, that's the excuse the majority of people use when they don't have "it" that day.

But it's not about some magic feeling of "it" or about always being in a flow state that separates consistent winners from those who aren't. Because what you *feel* like on a given day should be irrelevant.

It's about what you *choose* to do that day that makes the difference.

Competition is a *chosen* lifestyle.

That choice is made every morning and multiple times throughout the day. It's not natural. You may be born with competitive traits, but the behaviors that lead to becoming a Competitor are *learned*.

Being a Competitor has nothing to do with whether you like sports or not, or with whether you consider yourself "competitive" or not, or with whether you see yourself right now as capable of *more*. It has nothing to do with your genetics. Instead, it has everything to do with your heart, your effort, and your focus. Being a Competitor is about overcoming challenges, bending but not breaking from adversity, and seizing success.

It's not about a sport or a workout style. It's about an everyday lifestyle.

Being a Competitor is not about what you were born with but about what you build over the course of your life through your choices and actions. Because being a Competitor is a simple *choice*.

Yes or no—will I compete today?

It's a simple answer—yes or no. No "maybe" or "kinda" responses will suffice. You can't "try" to compete—you're in, or you're out. It's that simple.

But simple doesn't mean *easy*. In fact, it will be one of the hardest decisions you'll ever have to make some mornings. It will seem impossible at various points along the journey. And if you're anyone like me, you'll question if you even have what it takes to be a Competitor some days.

The truth is *you do* have what it takes.

It's there, inside of you. Embedded within you, while you were still being knit together in your mother's womb, lies a fierce, strong Competitor, just waiting for you to make the *choice* to let it out.

Some people discover that Competitor on a sports field, some in academics, or some in their career. They begin to seek it out constantly, looking for challenges to step up toward.

It remains hidden for decades in others, until life pushes them to a breaking point and their inner Competitor finally decides to start pushing back and reclaiming their lives.

And, for some, it remains dormant for an entire "normal" life, never to be let out and given the opportunity to show them how much *better* things could be.

Just like any skill we develop in school, the skill of *choosing to compete* is one that takes consistent repetitions over time to take hold and to help us become *who we are*.

But you're here, reading this, which means you've made the first step toward discovering your inner Competitor.

"Can't See" Creates "Can't Miss"

Our choices—more than our talent, our current income, and our fitness—determine our fate.

It's easy to think that it's one shining moment that changes everything for us.

That if "just this one thing" would happen, we'd be success-ful, just like others we see on social media or at work. But it's not the one big moment that made them successful. It's the small ones made consistently for weeks, months, and even years earlier that did make them successful.

- Our small choices each day add the biggest wins to our relationships.

- Our small choices each day contribute the most growth to our professional careers.

- Our small choices each day add up to achieve our biggest lifetime victories.

Small choices challenge comfort zones and complacency. Small choices help us build grit and embrace accountability. Small, seemingly *simple* choices, that when made consistently over time, create life-changing impacts.

One percent isn't very much to most of us. Ask any persons if they want 1 percent of something, and most of them would believe it's not enough to truly matter and would pass on the offer.

One percent seems small, barely noticeable to the naked eye. You don't initially notice a 1 percent growth in your bank statement or in your weight on the scale.

But what if you added that 1 percent today to 1 percent from yesterday and then repeated that formula every day?

Pretty soon, you wouldn't be able to *not* see that 1 percent improvement.

James Clear details the importance of a daily 1 percent improvement in his book *Atomic Habits: An Easy & Proven Way to Build Good Habits & Break Bad Ones.* Just as your finances can dramatically accelerate over enough time with a 1 percent compounding interest, so too can your successes in life.

If you were active social drinker who had a glass of wine every night, you wouldn't immediately notice trading that glass of wine for a glass of water. But what if you were to do that every day for 365 days? You'd consume 45,625 *fewer* calories in a year.

The one glass of wine that one night isn't a big deal, but it's the small choice to continue having that glass when you've said you wanted to lose weight. Trading that nightly glass of wine for a glass of water over the course of a year essentially equates to saving twenty-two day's worth of food at a standard 2,000 daily calorie intake. That fifteen pounds you wanted to lose? Problem solved.

The small choices to move forward start slowly—you can barely notice the 1 percent change, if at all. But the more you consistently choose the actions of the person you want to be, the more rapidly that growth curve begins to turn upward, until it hits an inflection point and skyrockets upward with the momentum and rate of a rocket ship.

Most would assume this new version of you "came out of nowhere, like an overnight success," without realizing you'd actually been doing small, 1 percent steps every day for years until that one pivotal moment when the compounding interest of your choices caught up—and you took off.

The *biggest* impacts you want to make in your career, in your health, and in your home life won't come from one magic moment. They'll come from thousands of tiny moments, instead.

Big "can't miss" impacts come from the smallest of "can't see" choices.

I Didn't Choose *That.*

Ask most people unhappy about their current situation, and they'll tell you that they didn't *choose* it—it just happened to them.

They genuinely believe that they didn't choose a bad boss, a failing relationship, or a struggling business. Ask them enough questions, and you'll see that they believe they didn't choose to have this current life; it's "just the cards they were dealt."

No people go into a marriage thinking they're going to get divorced. No people start businesses with plans to be bankrupt soon after. And no young and fit people ever think they're going to be out of shape.

We don't intend to fail in business, to have a relationship fall apart, or to let our health suffer, but in most of those situations, we've *chosen* not to be intentional in what our daily choices are.

We adopt this mindset when we passively float through each day. We clock in and out of work, we settle into a routine at home, and we tell ourselves, "I'm too busy for the gym."

When we do not intentionally choose how we go through each day, how we go out of our way to invest in our relationships, and how we block our time, it comes back to bite us over a long enough period. It's a slow fade—unnoticeable at first—and by the time we do notice it, it seems like it's too late.

In our minds, we didn't choose to gain fifty pounds—but what we did choose was weekly happy hours, late-night burgers, and consistently hitting our snooze alarm because we're "just not a morning person" or we were out "too late" during the week.

We don't believe we *chose* to let a relationship fall apart. What we did choose was failing to continually date our spouse, working with a counselor to communicate better, and investing in quality over quantity when it comes to our social circles.

We don't believe it's our choices that made the business go bankrupt. What we did choose was to launch it before we had adequate cash reserves, to spend frivolously in anticipation of "future" sales, and to worry about how great we looked online instead of how great our business actually ran.

We don't believe our choices at the moment will choose our fate—but that's actually what they do. One small, seemingly "not-a-big-deal" choice right now, when repeated enough times, creates a "big-deal" result for or against you.

You may not have chosen one big outcome—but what you did choose were the small, seemingly inconsequential choices that, over time, created that big outcome.

Success isn't about one singular choice—but about thousands of them made every single day.

Our Choices Choose Our Fate.

There's no conspiracy working against you. No tarot card is going to determine your destiny. And no astrological sign is going to guarantee your goals.

Your success lies in your choices.

Most people won't read this book. Fewer will finish it.

Everyone wants to be a winner. We all love to win. But the people who love to compete surpass the people who want to win, because the ones who want to win only care about the outcome—and not the process required to get there. Those that love to compete? They care enough about the process so that the outcome takes care of itself.

The magic of success is created in the process—not the outcome.

A study by the blog *THE IFOD* shows it's likely that less than half of the people who start a book finish it.

Most people won't put in the effort to discover the truth, because they don't want to know this one simple fact: to win at anything *requires something from you.* Success isn't freely given. It demands a sacrifice in order to receive it.

- Are you willing to sacrifice your long-held excuses?

- Are you willing to sacrifice weak efforts that just "get by"?

- And are you willing to sacrifice your comfort zone in the quest to discover what great work you were uniquely created to achieve?

The majority of people you know are entirely content settling for a career they hate and a life that falls well short of their created potential, because they believe that the comfort of their misery is safer than the road to their best life.

- They settle for small dreams, well within their current reach.

- They settle for toxic relationships, because being single is scary and unknown.

- They settle for a life less than what they were created to enjoy, because they've been tricked into believing that being a winner in life is only about lucky breaks that happen to "other people."

If you're still reading, it means that even though people you know have chosen to settle for less, you won't.

It means you're ready to learn how to compete every day in your life to be a winner at work and at home.

I shared earlier that I believe there is no one magic book or podcast or video that will change everything for you. It's true. But that one thing can be the catalyst that changes your mindset and that motivates you to do the work.

My hope is that this book becomes the catalyst that opens your eyes to the choices successful leaders make, while inspiring you to do the same.

As we take this journey together, remember this: it's never the easy things in life we do that make us proud. It's not the smooth seas that forge great sailors. And it's not the effortless achievements that inspire others about what's possible.

The work will not be easy—but it is doable. The seven lessons in this book will lead you to competing for and to winning success professionally and personally—success that most people will never experience, because most people *aren't willing to do the work*.

You still have to do the work after reading this book. But the lessons here will help you create the mindset required to compete for your best life and will equip you to make the *winning* choices every day.

Are you ready? **Let's get to work.**

Chapter Takeaways

1. Competition—intentionally forcing ourselves out of our comfort zones in the pursuit of something—creates opportunities for us to grow and to improve.

2. Most people settle for what they *think* they're capable of—which is always far below what they were truly created to accomplish. Choosing to compete every day helps you bridge the gap between what you *think* you can do and what you can *actually* do.

3. We can't reach our full potential when we're distracted by what everyone else is doing. Just like an Olympic sprinter, we run our best race when we keep our focus on our lane and our race.

4. Our daily choices—not our circumstances—determine our future successes and failures.

5. Your ability to reach your true potential and best life come down to what you *choose* each day. It's not what you're born with but what you intentionally build that matters most.

03

Outwork Your Talent

I still remember the first time I watched a televised March Madness basketball game. I was staying with my next-door neighbor while my parents were on a work trip. I sat in my neighbor's living room, watching Mississippi and Valparaiso play in the opening round of the 1998 NCAA Tournament.

In the final five seconds, "Valpo's" Jamie Sykes threw the ball inbounds to teammate Bill Jenkins, who passed the ball up court to guard Bryce Drew, who proceeded to nail a twenty-three-foot buzzer beater to send his underdog team to the next round—and send the heavily favored Mississippi Rebels home.

I was immediately hooked on March Madness. More important, since my team rarely if ever qualified for the tournament, I was hooked on cheering for the underdogs, the "Cinderella" teams, each year.

Ask any sports fans, and you're likely to hear that unless it's *their* team that's heavily favored, they'll cheer for the upset in any given match:

- Boise State upsetting Oklahoma on a trick play in the 2007 Fiesta Bowl

- The United States' "Miracle on Ice" win over Russia in the 1980 Olympics

- Mississippi State women's basketball team snapping UConn's 111-game winning streak after losing the previous year by sixty points to the Huskies.

Upsets reinforce the meritocracy of sports—you have to earn every win *on* the field of play, and on any given day, you can be beaten. Victory isn't promised—*even if you field better talent that day.*

It's natural for us to crave seeing a Goliath fall to a smaller, less-talented team. Dating back to the story of David versus Goliath in the Old Testament, people have clung to the hope that an underdog can win. From *Star Wars* to *Rudy*, movies and books share countless stories of the underdog successfully rising to overcome almost insurmountable odds. The belief that even the most talented can be defeated has inspired brave men and women to fling themselves into competitions: from actual battlefields to start-up boardrooms around the world.

Some believe that they have the pluck to be *that* one underdog who slays the more talented giant. But how?

How can a less-talented team defeat a heavily favored one with more on-field talent? How does a bootstrapping entrepreneur build a business that topples "the way things have always been" in an industry?

By preparing and playing smarter, harder, and more effectively than an opponent who is relying on talent and past success.

What if our successes weren't heavily predicated on our natural talents—but on the choices we made?

What if the likelihood of reaching our goals relied less on our innate ability and more on our intentional skill development?

What if we had the ability to climb higher, to achieve more, and to surpass our peers born with far *more* natural ability?

Competitors understand that talent is important but that talent alone doesn't get the job done. To excel, people must choose to outwork what they were born with.

Whether champions are highly skilled or have average talent, it's this underdog mentality that creates them.

Born versus Built

Sixty players were drafted by the NBA in 2006.

Jose Juan Barea wasn't one of them.

The Puerto Rican-born basketball player was deemed too short (five feet ten inches tall) and his foot speed too slow for teams to invest a draft pick on. Barea played a couple of summer league games before signing as a rookie free agent with the Dallas Mavericks. He wasn't expected to amount to much in professional basketball.[1]

There are a lot of teams who would have quickly taken a mulligan with that draft.

Since 2006, JJ Barea has played in more NBA games than all but seven players from that draft class[5]. He earned an NBA Championship in 2011 and has amassed over $41 million in contract earnings.

Not a bad career for an underdog player who was classified as "not talented enough"[6] to make it in the NBA.

Potential doesn't promise success.

How many talented athletes sit at home and watch less-talented athletes make millions of dollars playing in professional sports each night?

Thousands!

Thousands of incredibly talented players are born with the skills to succeed in a sport, but they didn't succeed because most of them were tricked into believing that their potential alone would get the job done. And when they realized otherwise, it was too late.

Talent doesn't guarantee winning, and potential never promises success. It comes down to what you do with both.

But how often do we forget this?

We open our phones, scroll through our social media posts, and can't help seeing others posting something great. They've reached a fitness goal, they've started a new business, or they're on a "perfect" vacation with their "perfect" relationship partner.

All the while, we look around and realize we aren't even close to reaching our goals. We hear those small voices in the backs of our heads point out our inadequacies compared to the "accomplishments" of those whom we just saw online. Remember the trap of comparison we discussed earlier? *It's real.*

That small voice tries to give us the "out" that the person we see online just has more *talent* than we do:

> *It's okay they've done so much more than you; they're just more talented. And talent is something you're born with, so you can't help it that you're not as good.*

In my twenties, I developed the negative habit of listening to that voice. The more I listened to it, the more I started to agree with it. And pretty soon, I had an "out" for the areas in my life in which I hadn't lived up to the standard—I just "lacked" the talent that others had.

- A business as successful as that guy's? He's just more talented.

- Can't build strength as easily while doing that workout movement as those other people? They're just more talented.

- Not getting as much online traffic as someone else? She's just more talented.

We buy into seeing someone else's small, single highlight online and compare it to our entire behind-the-scenes story. We fool ourselves into believing the lie that all others who are succeeding better than us are doing so because they have more talent.

Because that's easier than accepting our own responsibility for our current position, right?

We set a big, audacious goal. We start working toward it, but eventually, as in every pursuit, we start to lose steam. The work becomes harder, our passion dwindles, and the voices in our head grow louder.

Most of us eventually get to a quitting point, because we think that we are doing something wrong because we aren't "there" like those we see on social media or that we just lack the talent to actually succeed.

So we quit and leave "that" specific goal to those born with the required talent.

But What If?

What if you were born with the greater God-given talent—but other people were just harder workers?

It wasn't until a friend challenged me with this question that my entire perspective started to change:

What if I had it wrong?

What if I actually had the necessary talent—and the people to whom I was comparing myself simply worked harder? What if *I* was the talented Goliath—and *they* were the underdog with great drive? If that's the case—that I do have the talent—then if I find a way to match their work ethic, I'll fly past them toward my goal.

You can make excuses and avoid the responsibility of taking action toward your career, fitness, or life goals. You can chalk up someone else's success to pure talent and, in your mind, be devoid of the responsibility of having to outwork your innate ability.

Or you can be a Competitor.

Some of the most successful leaders you see are those willing to work harder than everyone else. They refused to let their natural ability be the differentiator on the road to success; instead, they chose to put in consistent work every day that built their future.

- That incredible weightlifter you follow on Instagram? Built through hard work, consistent training, and showing up every day, regardless of how he or she felt.

- That motivational speaker you want to be like? Built through hundreds of hours of practice, rehearsal, and giving bad speeches first.

- That entrepreneur with whom you want to trade places? Built through countless nights of little-to-no pay (or sleep), trying to solve problems until, finally, he or she found the solution— after failing to find it the previous 100 (or 1,000) times.

Notice the one common thread? It wasn't their talent—it was the work they *chose* to put into building their successes.

You get to choose.

You can *choose* to outwork your talent, regardless of how strong or weak you believe it to be.

- Born with amazing talent? Great. Outwork it.
- Born with average talent? It's okay. Outwork it.
- Born with subpar talent? No excuses. Outwork it.

Great talent is wasted every day by those who rely solely on it. But know this: what you choose to build will determine your future success, not what you're born with.

Law of Compensation

Journalist Malcolm Gladwell[7] was fascinated by the success rate of NFL quarterbacks on the basis of the round where they were drafted. Gladwell dove into an economist's research of the annual draft process that, to this day, still fails to accurately determine which quarterback will succeed and which will fail at the sport's highest level. Some of the best quarterbacks in the league weren't even drafted as the first quarterback the year they came out of college, and many weren't even first rounders.

Look at the rounds where these top-fifteen all-time quarterbacks were drafted and how many others were drafted ahead of them[8]:

- Tom Brady—pick 199 (round six, 2000)—six QBs drafted ahead of him

- Joe Montana—pick 82 (round three, 1979)—three QBs drafted ahead of him

- Brett Favre—pick 33 (round two, 1991)—three QBs drafted ahead

Gladwell makes his case about the importance of these players having to compensate for the pure physical advantages their counterparts were born with. He attributes the successes of these quarterbacks to the theory of compensation. The quarterbacks who aren't born with the same physical talents as their perceived "better" counterparts compensated for lesser physical talents by "working harder and being hungrier" to become better.

Just look at the NFL's 2018 top overall pick Baker Mayfield. On the surface, you'd assume that, as the top pick, he'd never needed to compensate, but flash back to his youth, and you'll see how Mayfield is a prime example of a player who compensated for a lack of early physical skills by outworking his talent.

Mayfield was smaller player in high school, and according to his coach, he lacked the arm talent and size that bigger players had.

"But Baker developed all the things you need to be successful before his body eventually caught up. His physical maturity, especially in high school, was incremental.[9]"

He received zero scholarship offers after graduating from high school, even though his team won a state championship and he was one of the top-producing players in Texas. He walked on at Texas Tech and ended up starting the entire season, becoming the first walk-on true freshman QB to ever start a season opener. Mayfield transferred to Oklahoma that next season, earned the starting job, and put together three of the best seasons in school history, finishing fourth (2015), third (2016), and first (2017) in Heisman Trophy voting.

Mayfield developed his competitive fire at a young age, and because of his late physical development, he was forced to outwork fellow teammates to earn playing time. Despite being a star in college and the top overall pick in the 2018 NFL draft, Mayfield's "outwork everyone" attitude was so ingrained in his mindset that he succeeded at every level. It's the definition of Gladwell's "theory of compensation."

Malcolm Gladwell argues that these two traits—hard work and relentless hunger—are better predictors of being a great competitor than being born with every natural advantage in the world:

> Being a great competitor in other words, is rooted in overcoming obstacles, not just capitalizing on every advantage you've been given. That is compensation—you took something away from somebody, and they came back stronger.[7]

The best in any field aren't born with the best abilities—they build them out of necessity. Regardless of how great or poor their talent is, their success ultimately relies on their ability to outwork it.

Effort Counts Twice

I grew up in a small east Texas town of 13,000 people. It's a small town like those you see in the movies, where the town practically shuts down every Friday night in the fall to go cheer on the hometown high school team. We'd pack into the old, steel bleachers of the historic Tomato Bowl and cheer for our town's team against a nearby town's team.

I remember falling in love with the game of football at a very young age. I'd watch Friday night games with my parents, then spend Saturday and Sunday watching college and professional football on TV. I couldn't wait to be old enough to play.

I realized I was never going to be the best athlete on the field within a week of starting Pee-Wee football. My dreams of sprinting past defenders or stiff arming them for a touchdown were dashed. There were a ton of guys that were bigger, faster, or stronger than I was. I still believed I had a chance to play.

Inspired by Little Giants

I was eleven years old and obsessed with youth sports when Disney released the movie *Little Giants* in 1994. It's the story of two rival brothers coaching Pee-Wee Football. Kevin O'Shea (played by Ed O'Neil) leads the Dallas Cowboys, a sharp-dressed group of all-world talents, the best athletes in town. The other team, led by Kevin's brother Danny (Rick Moranis), features the outcasts and less-talented, less athletic players.

The less-talented Little Giants learn how to play together, over the course of the movie and in the climactic final game use their strengths to defeat the favored Cowboys.

I always remember that movie because it cemented the message that my Pee-Wee coaches continually instilled in me: talent doesn't guarantee success.

Hard work beats talent when talent doesn't work hard.

I clung to that quotation, determined to be the hardest worker on my team. I studied the playbook religiously, I gave my best efforts in practice at every snap, and I practiced footwork drills and passing at home. My head coach knew how I responded to challenges, and he would casually make comments about the "more talented" quarterbacks above and behind me in grades.

His words stoked a fire within me to prove that physical talent—or lack thereof—wouldn't be what defined my athletic career.

It took four years of playing on our school's A and B teams before I was able to wrestle the starting job away from other players my age. Eventually, my grit, practice habits, and playbook knowledge won out over stronger arms and faster feet.

I always carried the mindset in sports that even if you were more talented than me, I still had a shot to beat you. I lived for the opportunity to prove that my work ethic was greater than your talent. In some cases it was; in others it wasn't.

I still believed in the truth about hard work and talent, but, after graduating from high school, I'd forgotten that it also applied to life outside of sports.

Talent versus Effort

In her book *Grit: The Power of Passion and Perseverance*, Angela Duckworth defines grit as "the propensity to pursue goals with a sustained passion."

It's the ability to go after your goals with a *relentless* inner fire.

How long are you willing to work for that goal you say you want? How often will you force yourself to get back up after being knocked down? How strong will your effort be day in, day out, even when you don't "feel" motivated?

That's grit.

Duckworth goes on to explain that our grit is *more important* than our talent when it comes to succeeding. She writes:

> Your talent is not the same as how hard you'll work. Talent counts—there's no denying it factors into our success—but effort counts twice as much [10]

Using our talent as the reason we have or haven't succeeded is simply the way we create an excuse to remove responsibility for our own efforts from the equation. If we can say we just "didn't have the talent," then we don't have to put in serious work toward the goal.

Duckworth's research shows that while our inherent talents are great, it's our effort and what we do with that talent that is twice as important.

Being the best isn't about your talent.

Even the greatest basketball player of all time understood this.

Before Michael Jordan was *the* Michael Jordan, he was just another really talented basketball player. Nearly everyone knows the story that Jordan was cut from his high school basketball team as a sophomore, but what you might not know is that the coach's decision is what fueled his entire off-season training to push himself to be better. He wanted to prove that he was better than his coach had thought, and he worked out every day to improve his game.

When he got to the University of North Carolina at Chapel Hill, he was a really talented basketball player. But what pushed him to becoming the number-three pick in the 1984 draft was what he did with that talent during his time in college. He practiced every day as hard as he would play in a game. He would make himself run extra wind sprints after a game, if he hadn't followed his shot to the boards for a potential offensive rebound[2]. He would practice shots for hours after games, never content to rest on what he'd accomplished up until that point.[11]

> The mental toughness and the heart are a lot stronger than some of the physical advantages you might have. I've always said that and I've always believed that.—Michael Jordan (from *Mindset: The New Psychology of Success* by Carol Dweck)[12]

He was born with talent, but it was his relentless effort that made him the greatest ever.

Another classic example of someone for whom we use "talent" as his or her claim to fame is future Hall of Fame NFL quarterback Peyton Manning. Manning was born to a former NFL quarterback and blessed with the physical size most teams covet. Many fans credit his success to his dad and his physical ability, but many other players who came and went during his time in the league had better physical skills.

Ask any one of his teammates about what made Manning special, and you'll hear about his work ethic. Manning was obsessed with preparation and with knowing every detail in the game.

He was religious with his preparation, and he wanted to know every possible scenario so that he could capitalize in any situation.

Manning would spend hours on hours watching film, many times being the only person left at the facilities. He would practice calls and plays in his hotel room long after his teammates had gone to sleep. He knew the place on the field where everyone needed to be on every snap, down to the exact yard line that a receiver needed his right foot to touch. And if a receiver didn't get to the point he was supposed to reach, Manning was known to have him benched.

He knew that the details were those which separated winning from losing, so he made sure he knew every detail. It's one of the reasons he was able to play eighteen seasons, even after losing some of his physical skills because of a neck injury.

> Greatness wasn't an accident with Peyton. You always got a good understanding of how important the game was to him during the bye week. He's still in there taking all the reps when everyone's relaxed. He's still treating it like a game week. —Edgerrin James[13]

Certain details that Manning would catch in film went unnoticed by scouts, coaches, and other players. But Manning worked hard to find every detail about the opposing team. It was the little things that created big opportunities for his offense, and it was his choice to be relentless in his work ethic that molded him into one of the best to ever play the position.

Even the greats understand that your talent doesn't guarantee your success.

Your effort is twice as important as your talent when it comes to success.

Talent Doesn't Determine Your Choices

Talent, as we've discussed, is outside of our control. We're born with certain talents and can't do much to change that. Our efforts and work ethic, though, are 100 percent up to us.

If we want to be someone capable of outworking our talent and excelling beyond what more talented people can achieve, then we have to raise our standards of what's acceptable. We have to raise our definition of what effort and consistency look like in our habits, work, and life.

We have to do more than what is required. We have to do it consistently every day, regardless of how we feel.

Tony Robbins shared a conversation he had with Michael Jordan after Jordan's Chicago Bulls had lost their third straight playoff series to the Detroit Pistons. Jordan was sitting in the back of the bus, crying and angry about another playoff exit. He wanted to yell at his teammates for not playing better and doing their job, but in that moment, he was hit with a realization.

Jordan said he was hit with the truth that crying, whining, and blaming everyone else on the team wasn't going to solve his problems. He needed to raise his standards of what an acceptable work ethic and drive were.

Jordan was relentless that off-season, investing countless hours in the weight room, as he had done never before. He grew bigger, stronger, and faster than ever before. He was committed to dominating every matchup and every second of every game that upcoming season. No one, he swore, would outwork him.

The best part? Jordan says it wasn't about competing against everyone else. "Everyone else was competing against me and where I am but I am only focused competing against where I could be. That's why I beat them[14]."

Your talent doesn't wake you up at five o'clock in the morning to go train. Your effort, attitude, and choices do.

Your talent doesn't make you coachable. Your effort, attitude, and choices do.

Your talent doesn't determine if you'll reach your full potential. Your effort, attitude, and choices do.

It's your choice to give your best effort that helps you prepare for that presentation weeks before you're supposed to give it. It's your effort that chooses your positive attitude, despite a rough month at work or at home. And it's your effort that chooses to do the extra work after practice so you can improve your skills.

It's your effort, not your talent. Because it takes zero talent to make the choices that create big results over time.

Effort Shows UP on Game Day–and Before.

Clutch. Adjective: the ability of someone who is able to make plays under stress and pressure.

Sports legends are *clutch*, because we know that when it's crunch time and the game is on the line, they're able to take over the game and win it. Our favorite leaders are *clutch*. We know that when everyone is stressed out and when that pivotal client project is due, our leader will come through with the idea to win the deal.

Being *clutch* is coveted. It means that you aren't overwhelmed by big-pressure moments, that you aren't distracted by stresses, and that you can be counted on when things matter most.

Sports fans believe players are either born with this "clutch" gene or not. Someone can't fail time and time again at the end of games and be counted on as clutch. Like talent, many people will say that you either have clutch or not, but it's not something you can develop.

Really?

Let's take a look at three of the best players who ever played in the NBA: Michael Jordan, Kobe Bryant, and LeBron James.[15] When you compare their "clutch" shots, as defined by hitting the go-ahead shot in the final five[1] seconds of a fourth quarter or overtime in the playoffs, you can see their stats below:

Michael Jordan: missed 53 percent (7/15)
Kobe Bryant: missed 77 percent (5/22)
LeBron James: missed 48 percent (12/23)

Jordan, arguably the greatest player ever, missed more play-off game–winning shots than he made—but would anyone ever consider him anything but clutch? Of course not! All three of these players are considered among the best ever—and you would happily put the ball in their hands with the game on the line. Yet it was never a guarantee they'd make the shot.

What Clutch Really Is

The definition of clutch—being able to make plays under pressure—is simply the ability to control your nerves in big moments and to perform how you've *practiced*. If you've practiced hard and prepared yourself, the nerves are much quieter, because you've put yourself in this position time and time again. You know what to expect, and, more important, you know what to do.

But when you don't prepare to the best of your ability, when you take reps off, or when you plan to "wing it," the nerves will eat you alive.

And you have no chance of making the necessary plays.

I remember being anxious the first time I was hired by a company to speak. A large organization from Houston had reached out about having me speak at its annual human resources event. I'd never spoken to a company before, and not only was I nervous about talking to the audience at the event; I had no idea what to even talk about.

"Just tell us your story and your company's message," the leadership reassured me.

I wrote down my speech, read through it on the flight, and told myself I was ready for it. But I wasn't *prepared* like a professional would have been. I nervously rambled. I paced. And I would consider myself anything but "clutch." (Thank God the organization asked me back years later.)

I remember the biggest eye-opener in my speaking career was the moment a coach taught me about the importance of rehearsal. You wouldn't go into a game without watching films, studying the playbook, and practicing plays repeatedly in anticipation of your opponent's moves. Just the same, skilled speakers should never step on a stage without rehearsing their content relentlessly. You need to know your stories and your stage movements, and you need to plan your speech as you would your playbook.

It's the repetitions in practice that prepare us for the snaps in games.

The more intentionality and effort you choose to put into your practices, the better prepared you are when the game-day lights flip on.

The difference between excitement and nervousness is your level of preparation.

The real difference between someone who plays bigger and someone who breaks when the pressure is on comes down to how that person prepared for the moment.

Being clutch isn't about your talent. It's about your choices to

- prepare for a future opportunity,

- outwork your last practice session, and

- give your best effort in that moment by focusing on what you control.

If you're someone who hasn't put in the work leading up to that moment, who hasn't visualized every game scenario, and who hasn't practiced repeatedly, then, most likely, your focus will be on the size of the moment, its stakes, and everything outside of your control. And you'll fail to capitalize on the situation.

But if you're a Competitor who has put your best effort into your practices and visualizing your success, then your focus will be the move you're about to make and what's in your control. You're able to block out the noise, the opponent, and anything that distracts you from executing the one thing you've already rehearsed a hundred times.

You know you've been here countless times in practice and countless times in your own mind. There's no nervousness, because you realize it's only excitement for an opportunity you've been preparing for.

Your talent doesn't make you clutch. Your choice to outwork it does.

How to Outwork Your Talent

Talent is great, but your effort is what will separate you from others in the long run.

Career

1. Invest in developing additional technical or interpersonal skills. You can listen to a podcast on your morning commute instead of music. You can sign up for an online course relevant to your industry. You can trade one weekend a year for a leadership-development conference. Commit to growing yourself to grow your career into success.

2. Invest time in working with a mentor or a business coach. Have someone you trust who can help you navigate the corporate workplace and grow within your role and organization and throughout your career.

3. Be on time. Every time. Be the team member your organization can always count on to be on time (or early) to everything. Reliability and punctuality require zero talent and go a long way in proving your value.

4. Choose to have a positive attitude every day. You determine what outlook and attitude you have. Choosing a positive attitude and outlook will distinguish you, over time, from your peers. The easy route is to let circumstances control your attitude. Competitors set their outlook and attitude on what they want—instead of on what others believe outside influences control.

Health and Fitness

1. Be consistent. Follow the programming of your coach or your gym or online trainer, and follow it consistently—not just on the days you feel motivated to. Skip the snooze button, and grab a jacket if it's rainy or cold. Show up.

2. Go all out in your effort. Unless your coach tells you to go at a relaxed pace or a slow speed, give your full effort. Cutting corners and giving weak effort won't make you better.

3. Hire a coach. If you don't have someone experienced and trained to help you get the most from your body, hire someone. That coach will hold you accountable, will program your nutrition and workouts, and will keep you growing.

Personal Life

1. Be a lifelong learner. Adopt the mindset that you will never know "enough" about a subject and commit to learn at least one thing new every day. Read a chapter of a book. Listen to a podcast. Talk with a stranger. Building your knowledge base every day sets you up to succeed much better than others, who are relying on what they know or what they watch on Netflix to carry them through.

2. Do what you committed yourself to do. Most of us make the commitment to start a gym routine—only to hit the snooze button each morning and push the routine forward to "next year." You don't need January 1 to change your lifestyle. You just need to choose to honor the commitment to yourself. Pick up the commitment you've been pushing off and make today the day you start it.

3. Ask yourself every morning, "How can I show up better today?" Challenge yourself today to be more present with your family, more proactive with your work, and more intentional with your time than yesterday. Growth is a gradual process, but we start it by answering this question every day with our actions.

4. Play the long game. Don't make sacrifices that damage your long-term development, relationships, and goals because of feelings or situations in the immediate present.

Build relationships—not transactions. Put in the work of building your professional skills, personal network, or health every day—even when you can't see immediate effects. Look at the big picture, instead of the small window of today.

Chapter Takeaways

1. Talent doesn't guarantee success. What you choose to do with your natural talent is what creates your opportunities to succeed.

2. Your biggest competitive advantage may be the physical talents you're currently lacking. Learning to outwork what you've been born with has created more champions than anything else.

3. Effort is twice as important as talent. You can beat more talented opponents in your work, workouts, and life if you choose to consistently outwork them over an extended period of time.

4. Your natural talent doesn't determine your choices—you do. Don't use "their talent" as an excuse to avoid responsibility for your own actions. Focus on how you're going to work harder than you did before.

5. Nearly all people focus on how they can be better than others. Competitors are focused on how they can be better than they are today, and they push themselves to see how much farther they can go.

6. Your effort and your practice are what prepare you for future opportunities to shine.

04

Never Let the Hard Days Win

Bad days are inevitable in life. Letting them break you is completely optional.

We can't avoid adversity—but how we choose to respond to that adversity is 100 percent up to us.

My best friend sent me a video of the 2008 Big Ten indoor track championship. It was a clip of the women's 600-meter final, which was a three-lap indoor sprint. It's one of those *lungs-burning, legs-aching* types of races. Three laps of no pacing, no slowing, just an all-out sprint around the track.

As I watched four women make their way around the track, one racer, Heather, started to take the lead. One lap down. Two to go.

Heather was holding strong to her lead, as the racers turned down the home stretch, preparing to start the pivotal final lap— when the unthinkable happens.

Slam!

Heather trips and face-plants into the track. The play-by-play announcers are shocked, and the crowd audibly gasps. The other races scramble to dodge her fallen body and keep running in the final lap of the race.

Failure happens to all of us at one point or another in life. For some of us, it happens in the biggest race of our lives, like Heather. For others, it happens on just a normal Tuesday: things suddenly fall apart. Failure is unavoidable.

But there's a key to failure that is too often forgotten. Failure is *an event*—it is not a person; it is not who you are.

Failing in the pursuit of something does not make you a failure. Everyone fails at something in life. All successful people have failed. They've struck out in their business, their health, or their relationships. No one you know is batting a perfect 1.000.

But we forget that. We get lost staring at the failure in front of us, believing it's now who we are, instead of the event that it is. And we forget that it presents an opportunity to grow.

Most see failures and challenges as things to cower in front of and to quit because of, instead of facing. Competitors see those same failures and challenges as **opportunities to rise up to and to show what's possible.**

How do they do this? By understanding that the most important part of any failure *is what happens next.*

After Heather nose-dived into the track, I expected to see another three or four minutes of sports-blooper clips. What I instead watched was a powerful reminder of how a Competitor responds to adversity.

Face covered in dirt, most likely embarrassed at how she tripped over her own feet on a flat track, Heather gets back up and takes off in a dead sprint after the other three racers, who are now a quarter of the track ahead of her in the final lap.

The announcers had given up on Heather, and fans were distracted from her, focusing on the first- and second-place racers battling it out. But as I watched, Heather started to gain ground on her opponents. In the back corner of the track, she passed the runner in third place. Two more runners to go.

I grew excited watching this old clip, as Heather gutted out an incredible effort right before my eyes. The crowd finally caught a glimpse of Heather and realized she was the same runner who had just fallen down—and now she was back in it.

Can you imagine the electricity in the air that night, as the crowd stood to its feet, screaming for the racers, when it realized that Heather was back in this race with under 100 meters left to go?

Heather ran at a breakneck pace as she gained ground on the final two racers. She passed second place halfway down the home stretch. You had to believe that every fiber of her body was on fire, screaming to slow down. But it was like magic watching her run—everything in her was working together seamlessly to produce this uncanny performance.

Then, in the exact same place she'd just fallen flat on her face moments earlier, Heather sprints past the final racer to win the Big Ten title.

Are you kidding me?

Heather Dorniden had fallen flat on her face in the biggest race of her life. She had spotted her opponents over a quarter of a lap head start on the final lap, and she had somehow gotten back up and emptied everything she had into running the lap of her life to win the title.

Setbacks happen in the pursuit of anything important. But to get from where we start to where we want to go, we have train ourselves how to respond to them.

An Olympic-Sized Example

One reason I love competition is that it's one of the few ways in life we can get a glimpse of our true potential. We always have more within us than we think we do. In a tough workout, you may be exhausted and ready to tap out, but once you hear your coach yell, "Fifteen seconds left," you suddenly find the energy to get a few more reps in. We push ourselves just a little harder than what we thought we had in us.

Derek Redmond may be one of the most famous Olympians of all time, even though he never won an Olympic gold medal.

Many of us don't recognize his name immediately, but I'm sure you've seen him run.

Derek was representing Great Britain during the 1992 Olympics as its fastest sprinter when he lined up for the men's 400-meter semifinal. The winners would advance to the gold medal race and would get a shot at making Olympic history. Just fifteen seconds into the race, he pulled up, clutching the back of his right leg. He immediately dropped to his knee on the track in pain. We later learned that Derek had torn his hamstring while running.

Everyone's attention went back to the racers finishing the race to see who would advance. As the camera panned off the finish line and back toward Derek, we were given the opportunity to see one of the Olympics' most inspirational moments. Officials and staff had hurried over to check on Derek, who proceeded to hop up on his one good leg and to start hopping around the track, continuing his race. He completely ignored another official who had stepped out to stop him before realizing it was futile to do so.

You could see Derek grimacing in immense pain as he tried to run on one leg around the track. He was in excruciating pain. Tears were rolling down his face from both the pain of his leg and the pain of a shattered dream. But he kept going around the track. I watched, wondering if he was going to collapse at any moment there on the track. All of a sudden, I saw another figure sprinting out onto the track, pushing aside security.

It was Derek's father.

Seeing his son in pain, Jim raced down to his side. He put his right arm around his son, and, with his left, he helped Derek brace himself. When Derek realized his father was helping him, he collapsed in his arms, crying. But what did Derek *not* do? He did not stop.

Together, father and son continued hobbling down the track toward that finish line. A security official tried to force them off the track, only to be pushed away by Jim. Derek was determined to finish that race and no one was going to stop him. One pace after another, Derek crossed that finish line in a moment that Olympics history will never forget.

Your response is what we're watching.

Unlike Heather, Derek wasn't going to win the race. He knew it the moment he felt his hamstring "pop." He couldn't outrun the competition with one leg, and in that short of a race, the fall had taken him out of contention. His placement was suddenly out of his control.

But finishing the race was still 100 percent up to him.

Despite being dealt a painful setback, Derek *chose* to leave *every ounce of energy* on that track, in an effort to finish what he had started years prior. It was slow and painful to watch at times, as he grimaced with each hobbling step, but it was also overwhelmingly inspirational. Here was a runner who had his Olympic dreams dashed in a snap, but he was still choosing to finish the race he had come here to run. Qualifying no longer mattered; finishing did.

He couldn't help the injury, but he still controlled how he responded to it.

It was not his fall, but *his response* to it, that created one of the most powerful moments in the history of the Olympics.

Our actions in response to adversity are what inspire others watching us. And, believe me, someone—a child, a friend, a coworker, a neighbor—is always watching.

When failure strikes, most often we don't know if we have what it takes to continue. Like Derek, we experience sudden, unexpected pain from a divorce, an injury, or a layoff. We want to crawl into a hole and hide from the pain, the embarrassment, and the moment. *"This isn't what I signed up for"* runs through our heads. We retreat in the moment, thinking we're all alone and that our world has ended.

But one setback doesn't end your story *unless you let it*. It's during our toughest moments that Derek's story provides a blueprint for how to respond.

Get up and keep running.

Get up and keep running for those people watching you who believe in you. Get up and keep running for those people who are going through a similar situation and have all but given up, believing there's no way out.

But most of all, get up and keep running for yourself *because your life story hasn't been fully written yet.*

Television shows end a season with a cliff-hanging story twist because the script writers know you'll come back next season to find out what happens. That story is left hanging midair, and you're left craving closure. *It can't end like that*, you think. The script writers know this, and they know your desire to see it end neatly is what pulls you back season after season.

Life works the same way. We don't want our story to end with a cliff-hanger. We want to end it with a strong finish.

We may experience a heart-wrenching setback during the race of our life. We may think our dreams are over. And we may have a lot of thoughts running through our heads in that moment. Complaining about the setback won't change it. Whining about the bad luck won't heal your hamstring or make a difference in your situation.

Commit to yourself that no matter what, you'll choose to get back up and keep running. Because despite the fall, it's still 100 percent your choice how you respond and finish your story.

Always Finish

During my junior year of high school, I almost quit football.

I was having one of those "off" weeks. One Wednesday afternoon in particular, I was in a mental fog. I misread two easy plays and missed passes that I wouldn't normally. I created a negative self-talk loop about my play internally—which, as you can imagine, doesn't help you climb out of that poor-play hole.

A study published in *Psychological Bulletin*[16] shows that our performance decreases and we do worse when we're focused on not doing worse. We stay in our own head, instead of focusing on making the plays necessary to pull us out of the slump.

My frustration was growing rapidly until, after missing another deep pass, my quarterback coach started yelling at me. I remember standing there as he ripped me for my play that day. He wasn't verbally assaulting me as a person; he was attacking my poor play. The words still stung deep. I'd worked hard to get to this point, and I loved the game, but in that moment, I wanted to be anywhere but on that football field.

I remember leaving practice that day with mist in my eyes, fighting the urge to cry out of embarrassment and anger. I drove home, telling myself that I was done with football after this season. I'd ride out the next month and then stop playing, because I knew I couldn't quit during the season.

You finish the year

I wanted to quit baseball when I was ten years old. I hated standing in the batter's box, and I wanted nothing more than to take back my hours at practices and games so I could spend them playing video games or riding four wheelers instead.

The problem was the time *when* I wanted to quit baseball. The new season was only a few weeks old, and I'd gotten a new glove and a new team. It didn't matter to me; I just wanted out. Fortunately (not at the time, I thought) my dad said *no*.

"You don't quit what you start. You started the season; you'll see it all the way through."

I was pissed. Like a brat, I threw a fit, yelled that "it wasn't fair," and stormed off. But he stood firm—Thompsons don't quit during the season.

My dad knew that my decision to quit hadn't come out of nowhere. It came soon after I was hit in the face with a baseball thrown from my third baseman during warmups. As soon as that ball connected with my two front teeth, I'd suddenly become afraid of the ball. I went from standing in the batter's box and swinging for the fences to stepping out and away, worried that every pitch was going to hit me in the face.

And this happened in Little League before kids were even throwing breaking balls!

I wanted to quit, I said, because I hated the game, but in reality I was afraid of getting hit by the ball again. I hated the feeling of being afraid, and instead of facing my fears, I was letting the fears dictate my excuses. I was trying to avoid adversity and fear at all costs.

Fortunately for me, my dad knew that—and he forced me to play through it, knowing that when I was an adult, I'd be faced with another fear and I'd have the urge to run from it again.

Unless I learned to face those fears at a young age, I'd be at a disadvantage later in life. I'd create a habit of running from fear after fear—instead of rising up and running through the fears.

Olympic medalist Nastia Liukin[2] once said that every time she would try to quit gymnastics, her mom would agree—but only *after* she had a great day at practice.

"Never quit after a bad day,"[17] she drilled into Nastia. Her mom knew that once Nastia had a great day on the mat, she wouldn't want to quit. If she still did want to quit after a genuinely great day, that was allowed—but she'd never be able to quit after a bad one.

Nastia's mom helped her develop grit by forcing her to work through her tough days, instead of doing what's far more common today—*letting her avoid adversity and difficulty at all costs.*

Her mom knew that for Nastia to excel in life after gymnastics, she would need grit, and she used gymnastics practices as the classroom from which to teach it.

The next day during my junior year in high school, I told my best friend that I was thinking about quitting after the season. In my head, it was a done deal. I would practice, ride the varsity bench for the rest of my junior season behind the senior starter, and then focus on having fun my last year of high school.

Thank God it didn't go as I planned.

Two weeks into the season that senior starter got hurt the first of multiple times that year, leaving me as the starter for multiple games, including a four-game playoff run, one of the best in school history. My last play that season was one I'll never forget: a touchdown run of over thirty yards in Texas Stadium.

I bet you can guess what happened next. I didn't quit after that season. In fact, I was more excited about the game and more focused on playing my senior year and potentially in college than I had ever been.

If I had given into my fears, I would've missed out on some of the best memories I had from growing up:

Weekly captain's dinners at Applebee's
Team touchdown celebrations
Going from a last-place pick in the preseason to a ten-win season.

I almost traded a game I loved and great experiences with friends because of fear and one bad day.

One bad day.

It's crazy to think about it now—giving up so much good just because of one bad twenty-four-hour period. Heck, it wasn't even a bad twenty-four-hour period—more like a bad three-hour period, if that. It's not the first time I've fallen into this kind of thinking, but why would I sacrifice something great in the long run because I was temporarily afraid or uncomfortable in the moment?

It's like the old adage—you wouldn't abandon a cross-country road trip because of one flat tire a few hours into the drive.

One bad day doesn't make a bad week, a bad month, or a bad year—unless you let it.

Adversity Is an Opportunity

Do you see failure as a challenge to avoid or as an opportunity through which to grow?

Most of us don't remember the process of learning to walk. We were too young to recall falling down repeatedly to take just one step. Eventually, we got to the point where we could muster two to three steps in a row from our parents before falling. Then five to six, ten to twelve, and pretty soon we were running rampant around our houses.

Falling down is part of the process of learning to walk. We didn't quit trying to walk after we fell down once or twice. Of course not! We picked ourselves back up and kept going.

I remember repeating this cycle when I took the training wheels off my first bicycle. The default option was riding downhill, because who wants to peddle uphill when you can *fly* down it? I started at my house, rode down the driveway to the left, and raced down the street into the nearby cul-de-sac, where the ground leveled off. On more than one occasion, I came flying off the driveway, down the street, and failed to brake properly, causing my bike (and body) to crash into the asphalt.

I didn't throw away my bike. I didn't care about the bleeding or scrapes I'd just added. I climbed back on my bike and tried it again and again until I was able to control the bike and execute a proper stop. The thought of quitting never crossed my mind—I focused only on what I needed to do differently so I wouldn't crash the next time.

I'm not encouraging you to go into your next interview, project, or competition wanting to fail. I am, however, challenging you to change your relationship with failure from something to be avoided at all costs to something that can be a learning experience.

We can't grow if we're constantly running from failure. We grow when we run *through* it.

The Bad Boys Helped Create the Baddest of Them All

One of the best teams in pro basketball during the 1980s was the Detroit Pistons—the "Bad Boys." Known for their bruising style of play and suffocating defense, the Pistons went to three straight NBA championships, winning two of them.

During those three runs to the Finals, the Pistons repeatedly knocked out another Eastern Conference team, the Michael Jordan–led Chicago Bulls. I shared earlier how Jordan responded to one of those playoff losses, but what I didn't share was exactly *why* he had to change his game.

According to the ESPN *30 for 30* documentary *Bad Boys*,[18] the Pistons physically beat up Jordan. The team had its own code of rules called "the Jordan Rules," which specified how it played the Bulls' best player. The "Rules" consisted of attacking him every time he tried to drive the lane and physically pushing him around so that he was worn out and beaten down by the fourth quarter of the game.

In response to the Pistons' bruising style, after he and his team were continually knocked out of the playoffs by the bigger, stronger opponents, Jordan transformed himself in the weight room. His teammates followed suit and transformed their mindset to match up with the more physical team. The Pistons players recalled that starting in 1991, the Bulls were no longer "the fragile, mentally weak team anymore. You couldn't mentally wear them down."[1]

It was only after losing to Detroit year after year after year that Jordan and his Bulls teammates forged themselves mentally and physically into one of the greatest dynasties in basketball history, winning six of the next eight NBA titles.

The adversity of a stronger opponent forced them to raise their standard and level of play. The challenges in life force us out of our comfort zone so we can grow into the person we were created to be.

The Midnight Rule

I've always been fascinated by baseball. My playing career didn't last much past my freshman year of high school, but the love of the game continued into my adult life. One reason I continue to be captivated by the sport is that even the best in it *fail 70 percent of the time.*

That's right. The best batters have a 70 percent failure rate.

The best hitters in the game fail to reach first base seven out of every ten times they step up to the plate. Average professional players? Eight out of ten *or higher.* In fact, since 1940, only *one* person has ever finished a season with a batting average above .400 (Ted Williams hit .406 in 1941[19]), and only *two* have hit with a 39 percent success rate since then (Tony Gwynn in 1994, George Brett in 1980).

Baseball is a game of individual failures. You can expect to fail almost every time you step onto the diamond. It's one of the reasons I love the game so much—it encourages resilience.

I once asked a professional baseball player how he could maintain the right attitude and focus every time he stepped onto the field when failure is so common. How did he avoid getting wrapped up in the cycle of failing each week so he could still make plays when he needed to?

"I have a Midnight Rule," he told me.

He went on to explain that whether he had a bad game full of mistakes or a great one full of SportsCenter highlights, he would give himself until 11:59 p.m. that night to dwell on it. He could celebrate and smile about the great plays he made, or he could yell and be upset about the plays he missed.

But at 11:59 p.m., he would let it go, because midnight signals a new day and yesterday's runs and errors don't carry over into today's baseball game.

"I can't allow past mistakes to linger in my head today. They build up over time, and, pretty soon, you're weighed down by the things you did in the past. Things you have zero control of now hinder your performance, where your teammates need you most—in the present. So, at midnight, I get rid of them."

The player told me that he would still watch films of past games for the lessons he could teach him. He would study where he could improve, what he could build on, and what lessons he needed the next time he took the field. Those lessons offer light, subtle cues he could use to avoid certain past mistakes and to compound the victories he achieved before. But he made sure to leave the baggage behind.

He knew that if he's constantly replaying the past, trying to change things outside of his control, then he would be unable to perform at his best in the present. Remember: you can't run with much speed toward your finish line straight ahead when you twist your shoulders and turn your head while trying to look at what's behind you.

All Competitors have their own versions of the Midnight Rule. For some, the time period lasts five minutes. For others, it'll go all day, until the clock strikes midnight. But all Competitors know that the setback is behind them and that when they go to bed at night, their focus can be only on what's ahead.

Constantly looking back at what happened *last year*? Let it go. Consistently replaying how well or how poorly you did last week? Let it go.

Because if you're stuck staring over your shoulder at something that happened "then," you'll be unable to perform in the present, where your family, your friends, and your coworkers need you most.

The setback isn't the most important thing that happened to you.

What Matters Most

It's hard to run at full speed forward, when our shoulders are twisted and our heads are turned, trying to look at what's behind us:

- The disastrous job interview
- A failed relationship
- Bankruptcy

Without question, we're going to face a challenging day. We'll fall short of our own expectations, and in many cases we'll fail. It's inevitable. We always have two responses in this rock-bottom moment of failure:

1. We can think about the mistake. We can replay it over and over again in our heads, mentally beating ourselves up about the "stupid" moves we just made. We can complain and whine about our mistakes. But none of those actions have ever been known to *change* the mistakes. Most times, they don't even make us feel better about the mistake.

2. Or we can choose to focus on *what's next*. We can turn our focus from what's outside of our control to what's inside it.

Call an Audible

A great quarterback is highly skilled at the art of calling an audible. It happens shortly before the football is snapped, when he walks up to the line, surveys the defensive alignment, and then either receives the snap of the ball to run the play that was called or changes the play to take advantage of how the defense is positioned.

In a few seconds, a quarterback must identify the key players on the defense and then adjust the play. Calling an "audible" lets a quarterback change the play after he sees and truly understands what he's facing.

A bad quarterback will just run the play that's called "because it's the play that was called" instead of adjusting to give his team the best chance to win.

We do the same in our lives.

We continue pushing in one direction because we don't want to change things up. We stick with the toxic relationship because it's comfortable. We stick with the unfulfilling career because we don't want to start over.

We believe the play that has been called (by God, by fate, or by our parents) is the best play, or the only play, to run.

In reality, we need to call an audible.

It's Not Sunk

Can you remember the last *bad* movie you watched? With this type of movie, when it finally ends you're actually excited to leave the theater. The movies *that bad*.

Did you stay until the end of the movie, or did you leave early?

Research shows that we are more likely to sit through a movie we don't want to watch because we have already made an investment in it. We made the time to get to the theater drove there, bought the tickets and popcorn, and expected to sit there entertained for the next two hours. We weren't happy—in fact, we didn't even want to watch the movie—but we felt we had to stay because of the investment (time, money) we'd already made.

We fell into the trap of "sunk cost."

"Sunk cost," in economic terms, is payments or investments that are never recovered. Our emotional brain tricks us into believing that since we've already made an investment in something, we have to continue using it so we don't "waste our money"—even if it's better to move past the investment.

We go to that fund-raiser even though we're sick and don't want to, because, otherwise, we feel like we've wasted our money. Instead, we could be using that time to rest and to recover in bed.

We stay in a toxic relationship because we've already invested months with this person. We sacrifice our limited time to in a bad relationship instead of using that time to meet other people.

We keep reading a book we hate because we've "already started it," instead of reselling it on Amazon and buying a new book we might enjoy.

Just because we've started something and invested time or money into it doesn't mean it's actually worth our continued investment of time and money.

We trick ourselves into continuing to pour ourselves and our resources into a past mistake, because we tell ourselves we can't have "wasted" time previously served. We keep looking back at that one bad decision (an unfulfilling career, a bad relationship, and the like) and fixating on it, instead of turning our attention to what's next.

If we evaluated situations objectively, all of us would quickly choose to start a new job, to end a toxic relationship, and to start a new path. But once we factor in emotional attachments and the amount of time previously invested in that job, relationship, or old path, we choose to live in the past and stick with it, because we don't want to waste the time spent before.

Start Your Engines

Imagine sitting in a race car at the starting line of the Indianapolis 500. You can feel the heat and smell the fumes of fuel ready to burn as you and thirty-three other drivers prepare to race around the asphalt track for 500 miles. The flag waves to signal the start of the race, but instead of launching forward, you keep your emergency brake engaged.

Your engine roars and your tires screech, as you press the gas pedal to the floor, but your car doesn't move—*not even an inch*. Smoke engulfs your car as your tires spin in place and burn their rubber on the track, but you still don't move from the starting line. Other racers whiz past you to start the race (and again after the first lap) while you continue to spin your tires, burn your gasoline, and go *nowhere*.

At some point, the pit crew is going to have to remove you from the track, because you've worn your tires out and used up all of your gasoline. Your car is a worthless shell without its tires or gasoline—and it's still sitting at the starting line.

Our lives can mirror that race if we choose to keep reliving our past mistakes in an endless loop. Like a racer burning all of his fuel to spin his tires at the starting line, we waste our limited fuel (energy, time, focus) by living in what happened in our rear-view mirror instead of what's ahead through the windshield. We choose to focus on what's out of our control in the past, imagining different scenarios that will never be able to change what happened then. We stress out, wishing we could change things (that we can't) or mentally beating ourselves up about things we no longer have influence over.

We exhaust all of our energy replaying our past failures, so we have nothing left in our tank for future pursuits.

What's Next?

If you move your eyes off what just happened, you can start focusing on your next move. You don't control the past—you have zero ability to change what happened *then*. But what happens *next*?

That's 100 percent on you.

New England Patriots quarterback Tom Brady was once asked what his favorite Super Bowl memory was. His response? "The *next* one."

Brady's answer is the perfect example of how a Competitor knows that what matters most is not what was, but what's ahead, because what's ahead is all that you control. Brady's the greatest player of all time at his position. He's won multiple championships and lost multiple ones. He knows the joy of winning back-to-back titles and the pain of missing perfection by just three points.

He's not content with prior successes or consumed by times when he fell short. He's fixated on the one thing he controls: what he does *next*.

It's not about your setback. It's about the lessons you can glean from that situation and what actions you take next.

Your past is a place for lessons and learning—not living. What matters most is what you do next.

How to Never Let the Hard Days Win

Competitors know every storm is temporary. They are intentional with their focus and attitude to never let a bad day break them.

Career

1. Show up early and with a positive attitude the *next* day after your bad day. Competitors aren't distracted by what happened then, because they're focused on what they control—what they do next. Show up early. Choose your positive attitude. Lead your coworkers by showing them a bad day doesn't break a Competitor.

2. Overlooked for another promotion? Invest extra time *after* work to learn new skills. Invest time with your mentor (or find one) to learn how you can set yourself apart. Do the extra work. Put yourself in a position so that there is zero doubt who's the best candidate for the next opportunity. Use the disappointment of being overlooked as fuel to build your better self.

3. Leave it at the office. Just like using the midnight rule to reset after a bad meeting, leave the bad day at the office. When you walk out of the door and head home, turn on your favorite music and just drive. Leave the anger or disappointment in your car so that when you walk into your house, you don't bring it with you to burden your roommate, friend, or family.

Health and Fitness

1. Never let one bad meal or workout or day derail your entire plan. Commit to yourself that any losing streak ends at one. It's easy to give into the feelings of "I've already blown my day with this meal; I might as well continue." But easy doesn't let you reach success. Put your foot down, and rebound after every setback by making the *next* one count.

2. Focus on your work. It's easy to lose motivation and to get frustrated after we fail to hit a benchmark that we *thought* we could hit. It's even harder to keep our motivation when we start looking at what everyone else is doing. Turn your attention to a) stopping the losing streak and b) knowing what you will do, starting *now*, to rebound. Don't let the idea of looking at someone else's work stop you from continuing onward with your own.

Personal Life

1. Avoid sinking deeper into your "sunk hole." Remind yourself that even if you've already invested time and money into something, it's okay to quit if you can better use that time elsewhere. Quit the book. Walk out of the movie. Your time is more important than your money, because you can always earn more money, but you'll never get back your time, the one resource that can never be replenished. Don't stay in the quicksand "because I'm already standing here."

2. Use the midnight rule after a bad day. Get into your car. Crank up Metallica. Scream at your steering wheel. Get

it out of your system. But as soon as you turn the car off and climb out, it's behind you. Commit your focus to the "now" and to being present where you're needed most. Use the renewed focus to *learn* what you can do next time you're in that situation.

3. Write it down. We all have past mistakes we want a "redo" on. We've dealt with that terrible hangover from drinking too much. We've had our hearts broken. We've wanted to run away. We've been *there*. Too many of us bring that incident from yesterday into today—we carry it everywhere. Remind yourself that today is a new day. Every morning, write down three things you're grateful for and then one lesson you learned from *that* experience. Be objective and honest. Find one lesson you can grow from or something you'd do differently next time *after* you've primed your thoughts with gratitude. Do it every day, until you find yourself at peace with the past.

Chapter Takeaways

1. Setbacks are an inevitable part of life. Competitors are prepared for challenging times, knowing that how they respond to those challenges is still 100 percent up to them.

2. Avoiding adversity never makes us better. Overcoming it does.

3. Some of the biggest challenges we face in life can become the reasons we grow into a person capable of succeeding. Like Jordan's Bulls, we need to battle our life's Pistons in order to forge ourselves into Competitors capable of winning.

4. Create a Midnight Rule. Give yourself a short window to celebrate or mourn the past. At your deadline, let it go, because the past is a place for learning, not for living.

5. What matters most is not what happened in the past, but what you do next.

05

Embrace the Process

There's no better time of year in Texas than Friday nights in the fall.

High school stadiums throughout the state shine bright as teenagers take the field with clear eyes and full hearts, intent on winning. Fans pack into those stadiums, cheering for that kid from down the street or so-and-so's grandson.

It doesn't matter what side of your town's railroad tracks you live on or what your mom does for work—the only two things that matter are the name on the front of the jersey and winning the game.

The key to winning Friday night's matchup comes down to what's done not in the few days leading up to the game but in the ten months before the game.

You don't show up on Friday night ready to play the game unless you've prepared for it.

What Really Goes into Game Day

Each year, two types of players show up to the start of preseason football training camp in August. One type of player is primed and ready to go.

Off-season workouts? They were the first one there, and they gave 100 percent effort every rep. Bleacher climbs? They were one of the few willing to show up in the cold and to sprint every step. Playbook knowledge? They've spent months memorizing not only their position on the field but where their other teammates would be.

These players are *ready to go* when camp starts in August. They already look like they're in game-day form, running crisp routes, knowing every play adjustment, and sprinting past that *other* type of player at camp.

You know which type I'm referring to, right? You can always identify this *other* type of player.

This type of player is standing with their hands on their knees, sucking wind, or they're throwing up in a nearby trash can. They're nowhere near game ready after spending the last ten months waiting for games instead of preparing for them.

Summer workouts? They showed up to one here or there, choosing instead to spend their time somewhere more "convenient" than the weight room.

Bleacher sprints? They skipped them, conveniently feeling "under the weather" every time.

These players focused solely on how they felt in the moment. They intentionally chose to do what was *more comfortable* in the *present* than what was *more important* for their *future*.

The players at their peak, ready to play? They were willing to endure the discomfort of off-season training, because they were focused on the game day that awaited. Every time their inner voice whispered to slow down or take a rep off, they'd shrug it aside, choosing to instead push harder, because they knew the truth.

Game day was coming.

The out-of-shape players? They submitted to that quiet voice, believing they had plenty of time to prepare before the first game. Missing a day here or giving half-effort there wouldn't impact how they played on game day, because, in their mind, "it was so far away."

They failed to realize the truth in sports: you don't shine on game day, when everyone is watching, unless you're willing to grind through the discomfort when no one else is. You don't succeed unless you're willing to persevere through the process.

Success happens over nights–not overnight.

Those "overnight success" stories in the media paint a picture indicating that some people simply came out of nowhere. It's as if they woke up one day, discovered they had a talent, and become known worldwide.

Culture will trick you into believing that success simply strikes certain people like a lightning bolt. It appears out of nowhere and is as rare as getting hit by an actual lightning bolt (hint: 1 in 700,000[20]). There's no rhyme or reason; some people just get lucky and get hit by the lightning bolt, and the rest of us don't. Culture will trick you into believing that "today might be the day!" Success can change your life—but most often will miss you.

In reality, success resembles an iceberg.

The top 10 percent of ice above the surface is what's visible to you and me. That's the success that others see you have achieved, the goals you've reached, and the posts you share online. But the 90 percent below the waterline that's invisible? That's the most important part of the iceberg, because that 90 percent of glacier ice is what holds up the 10 percent that can be seen. It consists of the days, weeks, months, and—many times—*years* spent doing the work. It's the time invested in practicing, rebounding from failure, and continually honing your craft when no one is watching.

You won't receive accolades for the 10 percent above the waterline without the 90 percent to hold it up.

Michael Bublé is a globally famous singer, known for his work in jazz, swing, and traditional pop. You've more than likely heard some of his covers of Frank Sinatra or his best-selling Christmas album. Bublé sells out arenas wherever he goes, and I paid a pretty penny to take my wife to see him in Dallas recently.

But Bublé wasn't always so famous.

In fact, as he shared at his show, his first gigs took place when he was just sixteen, performing in a nightclub where, as he put it, "No one comes to hear you sing. They come to drink and meet someone." In these nightclubs, with zero fanfare and attention, Bublé learned to develop his stagecraft. He learned to sing to an audience, and, more important, he learned to entertain in a venue where people weren't there to see you. In fact, you had to stand out for them to notice you. He was competing for their attention.

The more he sang, the more he learned to engage the crowd and leave a mark on their evening. The (now) famous singer spent ten years in relative obscurity, improving his ability to sing and entertain.

It looks like it's second nature for him now, as he delights and serenades thousands of fans each night—but I imagine that wasn't the case when he started. It was only by working his craft and building his grit by embracing the continual process of skill improvement that he was able to capitalize on it when he finally received his big opportunity.

He shone bright above the water's surface because of the work he put in below it.

We reach our "overnight success" by embracing the process over countless nights until our opportunity arrives.

What Really Goes into a Sixty-Minutes Performance?

Kevin Hart is a comedian, an actor, and a celebrity. His larger-than-life personality has entertained audiences around the world, but it's his work ethic and his relationship with failure that have made him great.

He shared during an interview[21] how he prepares for one of his tours by working the material for over eighteen months before delivering the sixty-minute set. Hart starts small, working comedic bits in tiny comedy clubs, knowing that some of the jokes will not work. He'll receive no laughs, or he'll receive that one awkward sympathy laugh from a guy in the back. He'll learn from how his audiences respond which stories work well together—and which don't.

Only by investing months and months in these small clubs, working and *reworking* his material, is Hart eventually able to test his material in a small theater. If it works in that setting, he tests it again in a larger arena. If it doesn't pass, he goes back to the small clubs to rework the jokes. Every story has to flow together seamlessly. Every roar of laughter has to be almost on cue. Every movement on stage needs to be locked in—it appears to the unknowing eye as if he's wandering on the stage, but Hart knows where he is standing for every joke every time.

He prepares for his tour in the arena, once the material is to his liking. He doesn't just show up on stage and drop a sixty-minute laugh-until-you-cry set. He invests months into the process of failing and getting better in order to create and to deliver that set.

Stand-up comedians embrace failure as part of their process to improve. They understand that only by going through those difficult moments can they create material that works. They step onto that stage, grab the microphone, and know that some material is going to land flat—and that an awkward silence is going to fill the club.

Make a note—*that joke doesn't work*—and move on.

There's no replaying of "*I sucked tonight*" or questioning their ability to tell jokes. It's simply making a mental note to remember that one specific bit doesn't work—and to remove it or to rework its delivery. And they get better.

Kevin Hart intentionally steps into the discomfort of failure on that small club stage in order to grow. He isn't concerned that he, a world-renowned entertainer, is going to tell bad jokes in order to see which of the jokes he's created work. He isn't worried that people may not laugh at his bad jokes. He's only concerned with figuring out which jokes they *will* laugh at so he can continue to refine them.

He doesn't care what others think about his failures, because he's only concerned with getting better. He's embracing his process.

It's Not about "Right Now"

At some point in my high school career, my mindset shifted from enjoying life to craving acceptance. I started trying to look perfect. I didn't want to look like I had to work hard for good grades. I changed what brands of clothes I wore. And I tried my best to "fit in."

I became obsessed with wanting to look good for the right people so I'd be considered "cool" among my classmates.

What starts as a desire to fit in with others can quickly become a trap. I avoided classes that could challenge me intellectually, because I didn't want to look nerdy or jeopardize my chance at an easy "A." I cared more about how I looked than I did about how I could get better.

This trend continued in college when, after getting my butt handed to me my first semester by an economics class, I changed majors from business to journalism. I told friends that I felt this different focus would help me more in my dream career, but honestly, this focus happened because I was afraid of looking dumb in business classes after struggling with basic economics.

I worry that today's youth have an even bigger battle than I did. The explosion of social media puts our entire lives online for the world to see, to judge, and to comment on. My most embarrassing moment from high school will live only in the memories of my teammates and my friends, who still laugh about it. Today's high school senior's most embarrassing moment? An online comment for her grandkids to see one day.

The constant online attention fuels this need to look perfect at all times.

We've created a culture that screams, "Don't stand out. Don't look like you're trying too hard. And whatever you do, don't do something unless you're great at it."

Most of us are listening to that scream. We don't post pictures or videos online unless we've edited them 500 times to get *just the right* lightning and angles. We avoid trying anything new, because we fear "what others will think if we struggle." We certainly don't switch careers or roles at work because what would someone say about someone *our age* looking like a twenty-two-year-old intern again?

Our obsession with looking perfect derails our ability to grow into better.

Your First Is Going to Suck

"If you're not embarrassed by the first version of your product, you've launched too late." - Reid Hoffman, LinkedIn founder.

I cringe when looking at pictures of Compete Every Day from 2011. Everything—from the photoshoots and shirt designs to our booth setup and social media—embarrasses me. It took a few years of consistently reminding myself of one truth before I finally accepted it happily.

Your first is going to suck.

We all start somewhere. It doesn't have to be pretty. In fact, most times it won't be. But you can't create something you're proud of until you just start to create *something*. That polished 100th step won't arrive until you start taking the first one.

Waiting until the "perfect time" will keep you waiting forever. Holding off until everything is absolutely perfect will have you holding off until you're dead.

The only way to build something good in your career, your health, or your life is to simply take action. Take that ugly, messy first step so you can take a slightly better second one.

If we know that our first step is going to suck, then we might as well get it over with, right? It's no surprise when we stumble, because we expect it and know that we're going to get better with each attempt.

Knowing that the first step is ugly is important, but it's not the *most* important thing to know.

What's Most Important?

You can care about looking perfect. You can focus on winning the approval of strangers online. You can invest your time into making sure every "t" is crossed and every "i" is dotted in everything you do before you start.

You can care about only getting better.

Only one of these two things will get you closer to actually succeeding. The starting line of life is filled with people fixing their hair and taking selfie after selfie in an attempt to get the *perfect* image. It's backlogged with those looking at their watches, waiting on a *perfect* time to start running.

All of those people will wait their entire lives at the starting lines, failing to ever run the races before them, because they *thought* that looking perfect was more important than taking action.

Life doesn't award medals for how good you look at the starting line. It awards them for how strong you run the race.

Worrying about what your teammates will say if you work with a tutor isn't more important than actually *learning* the subject at hand.

Right now, is looking perfect on social media more important than learning how to be great on video in the big picture?

Turning down opportunities to speak at your company because you're afraid you'll say "like" and "umm" may seem like a safer move in the present, but it will only delay any chance to establish yourself as an indispensable leader in your organization in the long run.

Embracing the process is about choosing to focus on how you can get better today over worrying about what others might think. Competitors care about how they can show up and do better in their work, their relationships, and their lives more than they care about winning the approval of everyone else. They know by focusing on their growth, they're putting themselves in a position to win in the big picture, regardless of how sloppy it may appear in the present.

You can care about what everyone else thinks, or you can care about getting better. But you can't do both.

Success Is Sexy

But the road to reach it? Not so much.

Success feels great. It's holding that championship trophy we've longed for or getting the corner-office promotion we've wanted since day one. Success is what we post on social media and talk about at dinner parties, because success is what gets the headlines.

You made it!

If success is a mountaintop view that overlooks clouds, green valleys, and a sunset, then the road to get there is a rocky, dusty path that stretches for miles.

It has areas of flat ground, where you feel as if you've been walking for days without any change in scenery. It has areas where you climb over sharp, jagged rocks, worried you're going to fall at any minute and have to start over. Just like every ride at Universal Studios, there are plenty of emergency exit doors placed along the way so that if you get tired enough, you can take a detour and walk through.

Success is sexy, but our road to get there isn't. Parts of it are mundane, other parts are tiresome, and some parts seem repetitive. We feel as though we've made zero progress at times, and at others, we're just wanting to hold on for dear life. It's only by consistently choosing to move down that road toward your target of success, one step in front of the other, that you'll ever reach the mountaintop view.

Make the choice to do the work. Consistently.

One commitment I made when I started this book was to write 500 words every day, starting March 28, until I finished the book or reached my deadline of October 22. Rain or shine, I was committed to 500 words every day. I knew from my research that there were two key things that would make my commitment to writing every day easier:

1. Forcing myself to make writing my top priority every day was the only way I'd ensure getting the book done.

2. Writing every day was the only way I'd ever get better at writing.

I'd be a stronger writer when I finished this book than when I started, knowing that if I wrote from day 1 until the deadline, I would have invested at least 208 days consistently writing. That's at least 104 *hours* I'd be writing if each 500-word session took a half hour to complete. (Most sessions didn't each take a half hour to complete, and I spent over an hour each day typing.)

Imagine what would happen if you invested 100 hours learning that new skill you talk about? Your 101st hour is going to look very different than your first hour, but the only way you're going to get to 101 hours is to start with one hour and to make time every day to work on it *consistently.*

YouTube influencer Sean Cannell once shared that "everyone's first 100 YouTube videos are bad. But the only way to get to your second 100 videos that are much better is to go through the process of consistently making the first 100."

We don't just show up great. We start ugly, we start slow, and we start, many times, with a stumble. Only by taking that crucial first step are you able to take a second, then a third, and eventually a hundredth. Greatness is found when a person consistently commits to the process, every day.

Competitors *start* because without that crucial first step, you don't get better.

Play Tag

I made a small mistake when I ran my first half-marathon in 2013.

I forgot to train for it.

"Forgot" may be a strong word. I neglected to make time to run. I don't even like running. I'd signed up because it was a bucket-list item for me to say, "I've done it." I'd picked Las Vegas because I figured that even if I hated running, I could still make a fun trip out of it, and the Vegas strip's lights and people would create enough of a distraction for me to prevent my ADHD from telling me how "bored" I was while running 13.1 miles.

I was working out five or six times a week, running 400 meters as part of my CrossFit workouts. I felt I was in "good enough" shape, and in my head, it was just a half-marathon. I'd be good to just show up and run.

So there I was, on a cool November night, standing at the starting line of the Rock 'n Roll Marathon, ready to go. I had my new compression socks on, my iPhone playing my playlist of favorite tracks, and I was wearing my favorite T-shirt. I was ready.

Flames erupted on both sides of the starting line as the announcer sent us off for our 13.1-mile race. I turned up the music in my ears and started running, weaving in and out of slower runners, trying to get away from the mob of bodies starting the race together.

I remember zoning out and just running. I felt good as I made my way away from the casinos toward the famous "Welcome to Vegas" sign before looping back and running right down the main strip.

This isn't bad. I bet I'm making great time. I have to have done at least four or five miles, which means I'll be done soon, and then I can get to blackjack.

I started to get a small pain in my side, but I forced myself to ignore it, because I knew I had to be coming up on the halfway point in the race. I kept looking for mile-marker signs to confirm my expectations, but I hadn't seen any yet for some reason.

My throat was getting dry, so I chose to steer toward the water station up ahead for a quick drink. It as there that I happened to see a mile marker fifteen yards ahead.

"Mile Marker 2."

Mile Marker 2? I have eleven miles left.

I have ELEVEN MILES LEFT!?

I panicked.

My mind was racing a million thoughts a minute. I noticed that the pain in my side suddenly grew stronger. Come to think of it, my feet were starting to hurt too. I knew I was in trouble.

What did I get myself into? My legs are already hurting—how are my legs already hurting?

I reviewed my situation carefully. To my right was a small barricade, and behind it, the blackjack tables and the bright lights of a casino. *There's an exit! If I can jump that barricade, spend two hours playing blackjack, and then sneak out by the exit down the strip, no one will know,* I thought to myself. I would blame a "chip-malfunction" on the weird timing and GPS of my race that day if anyone asked, and I could avoid what would be a painful couple of hours still left to run.

My brain was doing everything in its power to talk me out of the (unexpected) discomfort of running the race. I needed a plan "B" if I was going to finish this race somehow, because my own thoughts were betraying me. I had an idea.

Play tag.

Do you remember playing *tag* as a kid?

I used to love that game. We played it on the playground in my elementary school almost daily. One person is "it" and has to chase everyone else. Once the "it" person was able to tag you, you became "it," and you'd have to chase the others. We played a multitude of variations of this game (freeze tag, anyone?) every week.

The easiest way to win that game was to find the slowest, closest target and to tag that person. If you were trying to avoid being tagged, you would stay near the slower, easier tags so they would be "it" and not you. Or you would play along the outside perimeter of what was considered "inbounds" so you weren't caught among the clumps of others playing.

As I was panicking on the Strip that November night, I remembered that game and decided to play.

I would find a runner just a little bit ahead of me and start chasing him or her at a light pace. When I would catch person, I would avoid playing the race creep by touching the runner on the shoulder or back and yelling "Tag! You're it!" but I would mentally note that I'd "gotten him (or her)."

I would then pick out another runner just ahead and chase him down. *Tag.*

I repeated this exercise for the remaining eleven miles, until I could see the finish line and just sprint my heart out across it. I didn't walk. I didn't quit. And, most important, I kept my brain busy so that it couldn't talk me into giving up.

If I had focused solely on the finish line, I might've slowed down or quit. "How am I ever going to get to that finish line? It's so far away!" would have been my thoughts if I'd concentrated on just the outcome. It's the same outcome-only perspective we take when we ask

- How am I ever going to get to that amount of income in my career?

- How am I ever going to get to that position in my life?

- How am I ever going to lose that much weight?

We tell ourselves that it's so hard, so far, and so much work to go from where we are right now to that future finish line. Here's the thing: you're going to reach that future finish line in your career or health, just as those other people have.

You do it by taking one step at a time and by taking the journey one day at a time. You're not worried about what you have to do next Monday or at the end of the month. Instead, you're focused only on the work you're going to do today. Tomorrow, you're going to focus only on the work you have to do tomorrow.

Our goals are not achieved by looking at the finish line but by knowing where the finish line is and why it matters, and then shifting our focus to the one step we have to take today.

I would've mentally checked out of my half marathon if I'd just looked at the finish line over eleven miles in front of me. My brain would've talked me into quitting if I hadn't distracted it with a game of tag.

Our Brains Like to Talk

Our brains are incredible organs. Though they weigh only three pounds, they use 20 percent of the blood and oxygen our body produces. They are full of billions of neurons. If you pulled out all of the blood vessels in your brain and stretched them end over end, they would be almost 100,000 miles in length[22]—the equivalent of driving from New York City to San Diego thirty-five times!

Even more fascinating than how our brain works is how it perceives the world and relays that information to us. When I realized that I had eleven miles left to run after (incorrectly) assuming I had only six miles, my brain panicked. It started trying to talk me out of finishing, because it realized that the distance to the finish line, where I wanted to go, was much further than I'd originally thought it would be.

Has that ever happened to you? We start out after a new, big goal like

- paying off debt
- losing weight
- starting an entirely new career.

We're excited about this new goal, and we launch into the first day energized to save money, to work out, or to learn a new skill. Day two is still exciting, but our energy dips subtly.

As the week continues, our excitement and energy levels continue to decrease as we realize that the massive change we have been expecting to see hasn't revealed itself yet. In fact, hardly anything has changed at all. By the end of our second week, we review our current location compared to the goal and think to ourselves, *That's it?*

- *Just five pounds? I've got ninety-five to go!*

- *Just $300? I've got tens of thousands to go!*

- *I'm not as good at this as so-and-so. How will I ever find a job I like?*

We grow frustrated because the place where we are isn't anywhere close to the place where we expected to be. How will we ever get there if two weeks of solid work has barely moved the needle in the grand scheme of things?

It's in this moment that the voice starts talking to us. Our brain reminds us that the place where we're wanting to go is "too far" from the place where we are now. For "all of the work" that we just did, it shows us that we didn't get far. And the voice screams reminders that the road to our goal is going to be much more difficult than we anticipated. It whispers doubts, causing us to question if we even have "what it takes" to achieve that goal. Perhaps we should just resign ourselves to the fact that our goal isn't attainable. That goal is achievable for others—but not for us.

We start to believe that just maybe we should give up now.

The Gap

Our brain can talk us into quitting almost anything if we're focused solely on the *gap*—that chasm that exists between the place where we are now and the place where we're trying to go.

Most people give in to that voice. They use the *gap* and how wide it is as an excuse to not do the work. They stand at the starting line and continue to look across the *gap* at the end the goal. They buy into what the voice is selling:

- *It's too far.*
- *It's too hard.*
- *I'm just not born with the right talents to get there.*

They're terrified to take a step forward because they only focus on the *gap* and because the unknown terrifies them. It's like being at the starting line of a race and having no idea what's ahead of you.

If you want to train your brain to shut up in these moments, you need to distract it with a game.

Like tag.

Our brains can't maintain focus on the *gap* and simultaneously try to talk us out of continuing onward when they're busy with an easy task. So you give them one.

You pick a small, achievable goal—for me, it was catching that sixty-five-year-old runner in a bright pink shirt—and focus on getting it. Once you reach that goal, your brain rewards you by releasing dopamine.[2] You suddenly "feel good," because the brain is rewarding you for achieving a task. You feel motivated to receive another hit of dopamine, so you set another small, achievable goal—like passing that sixteen-year-old running in a clown outfit.

You *tag* that goal, and your brain rewards you again with feelings of motivation and goodness. More achievement, more dopamine.[23]

You don't get that feeling and motivation when you're focused on how far you have to go or you're listening to the voice whispering, "Give up." You get that feeling when you focus on small, attainable wins along the way to your own finish line.

It's not about "all of the" debt you have to pay off or "all of the" weight you have to lose—it's about asking yourself, *What can I do today to make a small amount of progress*—and then doing it. It's the same approach that members of Alcoholics Anonymous take to growing their sobriety.

Our biggest wins are the result of ~~one magic turning point.~~

Our biggest wins are the result of a multitude of small victories compounded on top of each other over time. It's small win after small win that keeps you motivated and moving forward.

Think about going to the gym. You grow strength by doing repetitions of an exercise. You work through your repetitions during a single workout, and they start to build one on top of another over weeks and months of training. It's slow and anything but an overnight change, but the repetitions start to add up until you achieve a new personal best in that lift.

You aren't stressed about maxing out on a lift six months from now, because you're solely focused on getting the best reps in *today*. You're following your training plan, you're giving your best efforts, and you're focusing on today's lifts.

You reach your big goals—and build your grit—by focusing on your daily reps.

- What's the next task you can *tag*?

- What is one thing you need to do today to reach that closest target?

- What do you need to focus on today instead of on how far you have left to go?

Competitors aren't discouraged by the *gap* between today and their finish line, because they're focused on just getting their reps in today.

Hope Isn't a Strategy

Did you know that 80 percent of Americans will have given up their New Year's goals within twelve days of the New Year?

That's right: by January 12,[24] only two out of every ten people will still be working on their goals. By the end of the year? Only 8 percent are left working on these same goals.

All others give up. They started the year with high hopes of reaching their goals—but no plans for how to reach them.

So how do we make sure we are in the 8 percent instead of in the 92 percent?

By having a daily plan. A daily *scorecard*, actually.

Just as in sports, you have to keep score to know how you are doing. I used a number of different daily-habit builders, daily planners, and goal programs, before adapting what worked best for me into the Competitor Scorecard below.

Download your own free version of the scorecard at Blog.CompeteEveryDay.com/scorecard.

Days of the week are featured down the left-hand column. Across the top is space for six daily actions, and the far-right column is reserved for the daily targets. Finally, along the bottom is space to write down one thing you're grateful for that week.

How Do You Eat an Elephant?

The same way you eat a bowl of Lucky Charms—one bite at a time. The six daily actions are tiny bites designed to slowly devour your elephant-sized goal for the year. Outline six goals you have for the year. I recommend three to four professional goals and two to three personal goals. Create a reverse timeline, working backwards from the end of twelve months to today. Example:

- To achieve _____ within twelve months, what do you need to do within six months?

- To achieve _____ within six months, what do you need to do within one month?

- To achieve _____ this month, what do you need to do today?

Big goals. Tiny bites. We'll reverse-engineer each of your six goals for the year into bites so that instead of trying tackle a giant elephant, we are *playing tag* with it.

For example, I want to speak to sixty clients this year. I know that in order to land one client, I am (on average) talking with five. That means for every five calls I make, I sign one client.

In order to hit my goal of sixty clients in a year, I need to make 300 phone calls—just under one call per day. Factoring in fifty weeks of the working year, five work days per week, that leaves me with 250 days to make 300 phone calls. Over one call per day, on average.

To align with my goal, my scorecard will show that I have to make two outbound calls every day, or ten per week. That puts me well over my average for the year, but it allots space for any missed days and gives me a buffer—I'd rather sign seventy to seventy-five clients because I made too many calls than to sign only thirty to forty because I made too few, right?

What if your goal is to read thirty books this year? That seems like an overwhelming goal to most people. *It's a lot of reading!*

But what if the goal was to read just one chapter of a book every day?

Much easier to imagine. We can knock out a chapter in the morning with coffee, at lunch, or in the evening before bed. It's just four to ten pages. That's doable.

On the basis of the average number of chapters in a book, if you committed to reading one chapter per day, you'd read over thirty books in a given year. But you won't do it by focusing on how many books you have to read—you'll do it by focusing on the one chapter you have to read today.

Every day, when you complete the action, write a giant "X" in the box.

Let's cut up your *big* goals into cereal-sized bites and fill in the top part of your daily actions.

Daily Targets

The right column features open space for three targets every day. These are the three most important tasks you have on a given day. Unlike your daily actions, which will not change throughout the course of the year, your daily targets will change every day.

What are the three most important things you need to do today to move your work and life forward?

In other words, if everything at work was to go to hell in a handbasket this afternoon but you got your three daily targets completed, that day would be considered a win.

If you didn't complete them, that day gets an "L."

One day, your daily targets might be

- Crush my board presentation

- Finish writing this week's blog post

- Review applications for a new team position

The next day, they might be:

- Schedule three coffee meetings with mentors over the next ninety days
- Write ten thank-you cards to past clients
- Finish a presentation for a new client pitch

Every day has different targets—but here's the key. Your targets are not your to-do list. A to-do list is that never-ending list of things that we think are important but that rarely move the needle toward our goals at work or in life. They just keep us busy thinking they do.

Your targets need to be actions that add value to your work and your life. Remember: if you get nothing else done in a day except for your daily actions and daily targets, that day is a win. When you complete each target, draw a red line through it, marking it finished. That's how you'll reward yourself with a "W."

Why This Works

In a team sport like basketball, there are moving pieces all over the court that are outside of your control. How a teammate plays, what an opponent does, how tight or how loose the refs call fouls—none of those are in your control. You have to play your absolute best, focusing on what you control—attitude, effort, choices—while dealing with multiple people and obstacles outside of your control.

The scorecard will work the same.

All the items you enter on the scorecard for your daily actions and daily targets are 100 percent in your control. You don't control if someone else agrees to a sale on Tuesday, but you do control if you make the necessary calls and ask the right questions.

At the end of each day, you'll review if you "won" or "lost" the day, knowing that you have the ability to score 365–0—and you also have the ability to score 0–365. It comes down to what choices you make today.

The scorecard is a powerful exercise for three key reasons:

1. **You maintain focus on your small steps forward** and not the distance you have left to run. Remember playing *tag* earlier? You're focused only on today and only on that one runner just slightly ahead of you. You're not panicking, because you have miles and miles left to go. You're tagging what's next.

2. **You reward yourself for taking action** every day, encouraging your brain to crave more of it.

The reason social media is so dangerous is that we become addicted to the reward of dopamine hits our brain gives us for getting a "like" or "comment." We keep scrolling (mindlessly) because we *need* more hits as a reward for essentially doing nothing. Our brain is rewarding us for scrolling with our thumbs, as if we just achieved a big goal.

Dating apps that swipe right or left? Even worse. You become more interested in the feeling of swiping one way or another than you do the actual person on the other end of that swipe.

Writing a "X" in the box for each completed daily action and drawing a line through each of your daily targets reward you the same way. Your brain is providing you a hit of that motivation, but instead of mindlessly scrolling through social media, you're making progress in your professional and personal life.

3. You create momentum, instead of waiting for it.

The psychology of momentum shows that once we realize a winning streak has started, we focus on maintaining it.[25] Once we accumulate multiple "X" marks in a row of days with completed actions, our brain begins to work harder to keep that momentum going. It also removes the need for motivation, because we're focused on the action.

Most people you know wait for motivation to strike before they ever take action toward a goal. The sit back and wait.

And wait.

And wait.

It's as if the skies will magically open up and a lightning bolt will strike them, sparking them with the energy and motivation to take action.

That conjures a ridiculous visual—but even more ridiculous is the belief that motivation just "hits us" and that it's at that moment when we should finally go.

In reality, motivation is created by action. We take action—even the smallest of steps forward—and our brain rewards us with that dopamine hit. *That feels good; I should do it again.* We're motivated to take another step, so we do. Each action creates more motivation. We feel more motivated, so we take more action. On and on the cycle continues.

The action precedes the motivation, not the other way around.

The visual scorecard and momentum will get you going, even if you don't have the desire to take action that day. It's no longer about how you feel but only about what you do. Think of an avalanche roaring down a mountain, covering everything in its path.

It doesn't start this strong or even this big. It starts small. A small snowball starts to roll (action). As it rolls, it picks up debris and more snow (motivation), growing in size and strength with each roll forward, until eventually it becomes an unstoppable force of nature flying down a mountain.

Just like that example, we want to create an avalanche of momentum that continues to create more and more movement toward our goals instead of just waiting in place for motivation.

Every day is an opportunity to move toward or away from your goals. The scorecard gives you a visual reminder of the day's progress, while keeping you accountable to move forward.

Be Where Your Feet Are

It's really hard for a quarterback to make the right pass during a game if he's focused on the place where he's going for the party afterwards. If the coach signals a play to him and he's thinking about the antics after the game instead of reviewing where the defense is lined up, the chances that he will execute the play properly are 0 percent.

Just the same, if you walk into a presentation with a prospective client and think only about what you're going to do with your bonus money after signing that client to a contract, then your chances of nailing the presentation and closing the deal drop dramatically.

You can't perform at your best in the present and maintain focus on improving in the moment if you're trying to live anywhere but in that moment. Part of effectively embracing the process is choosing to remain in the *now* instead of being anxious to get *there*.

I spent the most of my twenties in a constant state of rushing to get "there." I didn't care about the work I did in the moment, because in my mind, it wasn't the work I wanted to do. I wasn't "there," because I wasn't at the financial place I desired or as successful as the vision in my head.

I was constantly on the lookout for the next client in my consulting practice, because I thought that whomever I signed next could be the client who catapulted me to a new level of status and success.

I didn't take dating very seriously, because I was focused on my career and on what would lie ahead "once I became successful." I didn't want anything serious that could jeopardize my chances of "hitting it big."

I didn't even appreciate the growth I had made after starting to work out, because I wasn't at the same level as other members of our gym.

I struggled with constantly wanting more, because what I had right now wasn't enough for me. It didn't matter if I ran ninety miles nonstop in a record time. In my head. if I hadn't crossed the finish line at the 100th mile, it didn't matter. The only thing my mindset guaranteed was that when I did eventually cross the finish line, I'd still be miserable and unappreciative. I'd be let down that what I'd done wasn't as fulfilling as I'd expected it to be.

I wasn't enjoying the process, because I focused solely on getting to the finish line instead of on how I could get better today.

It wouldn't have mattered where I was in life with the mindset I carried at the time; nowhere I was could be enough, because in my brain, better lay ahead.

Looking back, I kick myself for how many great experiences and interactions I missed out on because of looking ahead, instead of being where my feet were. I trapped myself in a mindset so fixated on getting *there* that I never appreciated being *here*, my most important moment.

Because *here* is the place where we are needed most every day—in our offices, our homes, and our minds.

This Day Is the One That Matters

Do you have enough energy to win today? *Just* today.

Day one of any pursuit is always the easiest. It doesn't matter what we're attempting to do; we always have enough focus, energy, and drive to succeed on the first day.

First day of a health goal? We have no issues waking up earlier when that alarm goes off to get to the gym before work or eating food we'd premade for the day.

First day of writing a book? The words flow with ease; we have confidence in what we're putting on paper, and we might even trick ourselves into believing we'll finish well before our original deadline, months away.

First day of a new relationship? It's filled with butterflies in your stomach, fun conversations, and a great experience.

The first day is *easy*.

It's the ones after that makes everything difficult. Our snooze button sounds much sweeter on day ten, so we sleep in and skip our workout. Day fifteen of writing feels like drowning in quicksand, as you stare at a blinking cursor on your screen and can't think of anything to write. Day thirty of your relationship comes with an argument that escalates quickly, and now you're in trouble, with genuinely no idea of what you did or said that was wrong.

If only every day of the process to reach our goals could be like the first day.

Day One

"One day" is an unknown point in the future. It could be tomorrow. It could be next year. It could be what it most commonly is, "never." But Day one, that's a whole different animal.

Day one is the starting point. We all know what our first day is, because we've got that endless supply of energy for it.

We can stay motivated throughout the process when we shift our focus from how far we have to go to what we have to get done on day one. It's our end point to focus on. We aren't distracted by what's behind us—nor are we worried about what tomorrow has ahead. We dial in our focus on today.

But I won't accomplish everything today.

I know that's what you're thinking. There's a lot to do. There always is. There are a ton of runners ahead that you can pick out to chase. You need only one to start the game, though.

You only need today to get going.

Our first day is easy, because we have a fresh perspective, we're focused on the moment, and we're not worried about how far we have left to go.

We care only about day one.

We're able to maintain our motivation today and competitive edge throughout day one when we know how far we have left to go. It's the difference between going for a run until you're tired and going to run three laps.

You'll run those three laps harder and stronger than you will if you're told to "just run," because you know where the end is. Similarly, our grit is enhanced when we have the end in sight. We can grind and push through all of the discomfort when we know there is an end point.

We wear ourselves out mentally when we look at how far we have left to go. But rarely are we distracted by the distance on the first day. We know it's the start, so we aren't expecting to achieve everything instantly, and we're motivated to get moving. We wear out mentally and physically on later days, when we become frustrated that we haven't gotten as far as we'd hoped we would be by now.

But we're never worn out on day one of the process.

What if we woke up every morning with the mindset that today was the first day? Yesterday's wins or losses are gone. Tomorrow's work is still out of focus. We can't change the past, and the only way to control the future is through the actions we take today. We remove our focus from how far we have to go from our goal, and we start a fresh game of tag, because today *is day one*.

Day ten is hard. Day fifty will be challenging. But day one? We know we can win that one. All of us have what it takes to win day one.

If you want to embrace the process of improving every day, choose to make every day "day one." Remind yourself that anyone, including you, has what it takes to win day one.

How to Embrace the Process
Build the 90 percent base of your iceberg without an audience so that when your opportunity arrives, no one will be able to miss the 10 percent shining above the water.

Career
1. Invest time once a week to learn new skills related to your work. Develop your presentation (public speaking) skills. Learn new sales techniques. Teach yourself basic coding. There are countless online programs (free or paid) that teach valuable skills—if you'll commit the time. Don't concern yourself with the idea of starting over or being new—focus on how you're going to add another arrow to your professional quiver of skills.

2. Use the Competitor scorecard to identify what daily actions you can score yourself on every day: sales calls, customer follow-ups, social media posts. Identify the *most important* task to growing your career, and commit to taking a step every day.

3. Be proactive in building your career. Bosses don't "just give out" raises—you need to earn it. Be consistent and positive, and do your best work every time in order to position yourself as a valuable asset to your organization. Make the everyday small "can't see" choices that your coworkers won't see, in order to have the "can't miss" successes over time.

Health and Fitness

1. Eyes off the scale. Eyes on what you're doing today. Don't worry about what the number on the scale says—show up and give your best effort toward today's meals and workouts. The results will take care of themselves.

2. Hire a coach or pay for programming (gym or individual). Follow every detail, every day. Don't add to what's prescribed or cut corners. Don't stress if you don't see massive results within a week. Focus on doing the work every day. Look at your results over six to eight months, not six to eight days.

3. Choose the healthy food when you're craving a pizza. Go to the gym on the days you don't have the motivation to do so. Train yourself to choose what's important over what you feel right now.

Personal Life

1. Adopt a "day one" mindset with your most important journey—maintaining your health, writing a book, starting a business, or nurturing a relationship. Remind yourself that today is the first day, and then act accordingly in your effort, actions, and attitude.

2. Don't let social media distract you or cause you to compare yourself to someone else. Keep your eyes focused on

your lane. Unfollow accounts that you mentally struggle to see succeed. Set safeguards on your computer to limit your social media use. The only journey that matters is the one you're on.

3. On that same note, remind yourself that this isn't a high school popularity contest. You can choose to try to get everyone to like you (they won't), or you can choose to get better. Choose the latter. It doesn't matter what other people think or say—most aren't thinking about us, and the ones who say something rarely matter. Blinders on, headphones in, with your music turned up. Focus on your actions today and what you'll do to get better.

Chapter Takeaways

1. Success is achieved by doing the work to be ready to maximize our opportunities long before those opportunities ever arrive. You can't seize the moment when it arrives unless you've prepared for it. It's too late to prepare for it when the moment arrives.

2. The moments of success that we see others achieve but that we don't achieve are the result of the work they put in that we didn't. Success is an iceberg—and it's only by committing to the process of improvement over time that we're able to build the 90 percent of ice below the surface that holds up the 10 percent above it.

3. You can choose to always look perfect and to never struggle in front of others. You can also choose to get better. But you can't choose both.

4. You eat an elephant the same way that you eat a bowl of Lucky Charms cereal—one bite at a time. Our biggest goals are achieved by creating a process of consistently doing one small thing every day.

5. You win half of the battle before the battle has even begun when you choose to take action on the days you don't feel motivated. Simply starting puts you ahead of most people, who will wait to feel motivated before they act.

6. Focus on making today your "day one," every day.

06

Build Your Starting Lineup

If you were to assemble a team of five people to put on the field of life, what would your starting lineup look like? What characteristics would you use to describe them?

Are they people who enthusiastically go after every day? Are they people who are striving for success in their work and life? Are they people that care only about doing just enough to get by?

If you were to evaluate your five *closest* friends, how would you describe them? Would they share all of the same qualities as your "dream team" or not?

Are they people with whom you've intentionally chosen to journey through life? Are they people you work out with, work with, or go to church with every week? Or are they people you didn't choose but just met at a happy hour and feel stuck to consistently see?

It's easy to go through life and hang out with the people whose friendships we just happened upon. Those that we randomly meet at the gym, through social outings, or at sporting events. The more we hang out with them, the more we start to notice certain aspects of their life that we don't necessarily agree with. Maybe we question how they treat their spouses or how they only talk about doing big things but never seem to find the time to actually do things. Our sheer proximity initiates the relationship, and soon we find ourselves hanging out regularly, but there was never any intention in building that friendship. They're nice people, but if we're honest, they're not people with whom we'd choose to go into life's battles.

Yet because it's convenient, we frequently continue to spend time with them.

In sports and in our professional lives, our teammates are chosen for us. One plays sports with those who live in the same area during grade school. Coaches recruit players to build their teams at the college level. Human resources recruits and staffs their companies at the corporate level. You enter each atmosphere and learn how to work or play with those put on your team.

The only time I ever chose my teammates in sports happened during our seventh grade passing-league draft. I was one of eight captains and drafted the players I wanted on my team. Outside of that one experience, every teammate I had in sports was out of my control. My coaches (and small-town city limits) determined who played on our teams.

But in life, it works much differently—even though most of us don't realize it.

We float through life with the friendships we happen across. We meet people at the gym, in our neighborhood, or at work and start hanging out with them because of our consistent proximity. We didn't *choose* the relationships, but we just happened to build them.

This common type of intentional relationship building happens because of our inclination to choose spending time with people with whom we are familiar and whom we see most often. A group of researchers studied[1] how proximity influenced friendships and determined that many of us settle for relationships that are near us, because their proximity creates a feeling of convenience.

We choose convenience and comfort, because many times what's best for us requires more effort in finding, creating, and cultivating. What's *easiest for us* isn't always what's best for us, though.

If our growth and our success in life require intentionality in our choices, then we must apply the same reasoning to our relationships. Having healthy, enriching relationships doesn't just happen—they're grown over time. We may not ever choose our teammates in our job or in our sport, but we always get to choose our friends.

You don't get to choose your teammates in sports, but you retain 100 percent control of them in your life. The choices of whom you put on your team—your starting five—are some of the most crucial decisions you'll make in life.

Your lineup will make or break you.

Your friends determine your effectiveness.

Motivational speaker Jim Rohn famously said, "You are the average of the five people you spend the most time with."[26] If you are investing time with other like-minded individuals who are growing, you'll naturally continue to grow and excel.

The worst thing you can have happen is to look around the five people you spend the most time with and realize that you are the "top dog" in your group. If you see that you are the only person doing work to improve your career and health and the only one concerned about growing in your circle, then *find* a new circle.

Quickly!

You never want to be the person most achieving, most successful, and most committed to growth in your circle, because if what Jim Rohn said is accurate, then the law of averages kicks in, and your circle will drag you down toward them.

You can't hang out only with people who are comfortable and complacent and still expect to grow and succeed.

Successful Competitors look for groups in which they are in the middle to bottom so that the people with whom they spend time will force them to grow in order to keep up. There's an ancient Jewish proverb that says, "As iron sharpens iron, so does one man sharpen another."

An ancient blacksmith would forge iron into weapons through a process that combined extreme heat and pounding to work the malleable iron into a useful tool. Iron would then be rubbed together to sharpen its edges, making it more effective. The proverb speaks to the truth that the right relationships will sharpen you—making you more useful.

And the wrong relationships can just as easily dull you.

You need relationships that sharpen you in order to be your most effective as a Competitor. Your friendships determine your effectiveness.

Loud Doesn't Equal Important

Speaking as one of them, sports fans can be the worst. There are incidents every year at sporting events between fans and athletes. Most can be traced back to entitled fans who believe they can say whatever they want to athletes because of how expensive their courtside seats were.

I've never heard more profane things yelled at someone than the time I sat in the University of Tennessee student section for a home game against the University of Florida. I blushed hearing the words hurled at the Florida kicker standing on the sidelines. I was even more surprised to see that those words came out of the mouth of a college freshman seated just down the row from me.

Athletes hear some of the worst things ever yelled during their games. Outside of a few on-court or sideline incidents that escalate, most of these obscenities are never acknowledged by the players. How can someone hear certain curse words yelled about their mother, their dog, their play, and the like and still not yell back in retaliation?

Because the athletes realize that what's yelled from the stands doesn't matter as much as their play on the field. Most athletes learn from a young age that what a fan screams at you during the course of the game has no bearing on the actual game.

Yelling back at the fans won't change their opinions of you, and the sweetest revenge is silencing those screaming fans by making successful plays on the field.

You can't yell about how bad some athletes suck when they completely dominate on the field in front of you.

The sidelines are for cowards

One of my favorite quotations comes from a speech by Theodore Roosevelt:

> It is not the critic who counts; not the man who points out how the strong man stumbles, or where the doer of deeds could have done them better. **The credit belongs to the man who is actually in the arena,** whose face is marred by dust and sweat and blood; who strives valiantly; who errs, who comes short again and again, because there is no effort without error and shortcoming; but who does actually strive to do the deeds; who knows great enthusiasms, the great devotions; **who spends himself in a worthy cause;** who at the best knows in the end the triumph of high achievement, and who at the worst, if he fails, at least fails while daring greatly, **so that his place shall never be with those cold and timid souls who neither know victory nor defeat.**[27]

The person willing to courageously step into life's competition and to risk failure in the pursuit of something bigger is better off in the long run than the timid souls who will never know what it feels like to win or to lose.

There are timid souls all around you. They are the ones we pass in the supermarket, at the gym, and maybe even in our social circles. They live the life of complacency and comfort, too afraid to ever take action toward what they desire. They go through their entire lives and never once risk action for their best interests.

These souls will sit in the stands and judge those on the field. They mock the ones willing to put themselves out there. They laugh when they stumble. And they sneer when they succeed, dismissing it as "luck."

Those in the stands fear stepping into life's arena because they've fooled themselves into believing that it is better and safer to stay in their comfort zones in the stands than going out on the field (where they might lose).

And, one day, they'll reach the end of their lives and wonder what happened, believing that they just weren't "lucky enough" to reach the type of success they dreamed about. They'll blame others for their shortcomings. They'll die full of regrets.

Are you really choosing to listen to the jeers and criticism from these people? The ones who have never stepped foot on the field always have the loudest opinions for those who are actually on the field.

Just like in sports, their opinions have zero influence on the outcome—unless you choose to listen to them.

Being in the competition doesn't guarantee you'll win it.

That's the beauty of competition. You aren't promised to walk out unscathed when you step into the arena of life. You're going to pick up a bruise or two. It's a given that at some point you're going to fail.

Without the risk of failure, you don't have the opportunity to rise up and win.

There would be no possibility for glory without the struggle to overcome. Leave the sidelines and stands to cowards and their comfort zones. Give me the Competitors willing to get onto the field.

I want my life stocked with those flawed people who will bet on themselves. The ones whom life will punch in the mouth and yet who will keep getting back up and trying again. I want my roster loaded with the ones who abandon their comfort zones to risk the glory of reaching their best lives.

The people on life's competition floor aren't the ones insulting you. They're the ones who know how hard the struggle is, because, like you, they're facing it. They're the ones cheering your successes, because they see it as an opportunity for them to win. They're too busy competing to insult anyone else who is brave enough to compete.

As Brené Brown so eloquently shared in her Netflix special *The Call to Courage*,

> If you are not in the arena getting your ass kicked on occasion, I am not interested in or open to your feedback about my work. Period.[28]

The people insulting and criticizing you are never the ones in life's competition. They're not doing bigger and better things than you. In fact, it's the opposite. Those who are yelling obscenities from the sidelines are almost always the ones doing *far less* than you.

The best players in sports don't allow what's yelled from the stands to take their focus away from what they do on the court, and the best Competitors in life don't let the critics in the stands distract them from doing what it takes to reach their best lives.

The stands are for cowards. Competitors live on the arena floor.

Your Friends Determine Your Fate

The Saban Way

Alabama head football coach Nick Saban is notorious for what he looks for in the players he recruits. The coach's requirements by position date back to a list initially compiled in the 1960s by legendary personnel director Gil Brandt of the Dallas Cowboys. As he documented in his book *4th and Goal Every Day: Alabama's Relentless Pursuit of Perfection*,[29] author Phil Savage shares that Saban can identify a player by the way he walks down the hall and can determine if he'll be a fit for his program. He has a standard height-and-weight combination for every position.

He evaluates size, mobility, and demeanor for every player that he may invest time to recruit. The player *has* to fit a specific physical and movement standard for his approval and for the opportunity to join the Alabama Crimson Tide. You can't argue with his results. From 2008 through 2018, Saban's teams have a combined winning record of 142-15,[30] with five national championships in eight attempts.

He's arguably the best coach in college football, because he knows exactly what to look for in his team's players.

Successful Competitors know exactly what to avoid and what to look for when building their teammates in life, too.

If you recruit the type of friends who fit the model, you'll put yourself in a position to win every year, as Saban's football teams do. Your friends influence your fate.

Three to Avoid

Successful relationships are built on trust, communication, and support. These key characteristics are integral to successful relationships, whether you're investing to develop a romantic, platonic, or working relationship. Just as you want to find people who exhibit Competitor traits, there are also traits you should see as warning signs from which to run.

The "Yes Men"

You can hear the "yes men" coming from a mile away. They'll always agree with you—even if it's not in either of your best interests—because more than anything, they want to be accepted. Hollywood glamorizes this individual in movies, someone constantly following celebrities everywhere, agreeing with everything the celebrities say. The relationship is solely built on them constantly agreeing with you and keeping you happy so that you'll continue to keep them around. They avoid conflict and always find a way to tell you what you want to hear.

The "yes men" never have your best interests at heart, and they don't love you enough to tell you the truth or to hold you accountable, because either could jeopardize their status in your "in crowd." As much as we want someone to always tell us what we want to hear, a true friend is willing to sometimes tell us what we *need* to hear, even if it's unpleasant.

Faithful are the wounds of a friend, but the kisses of an enemy are lavish and deceitful.—Ancient proverb

If your relationship with someone is solely about that person agreeing with you and telling you "yes," you'll need to tell that relationship "no," if you want to succeed.

The "Envious."

Have you ever told friends about something amazing that happened to you, only to have them force themselves to act happy?

Jealousy is an ugly color on anyone—and has no place in a Competitor's life.

The second type of people to avoid are the envious. They see your growth and success as a threat to their own well-being. They will always appear to be good friends, at first—but if you ever bring up a promotion from work or a PR you earned at the gym, their attitudes will turn sour. They quietly trash-talk all those who are putting themselves out there to try to succeed.

Without fail, they'll soon start trash-talking you, *their friend*, when their resentment toward you grows to a boiling point because of your consistent growth and success.

The envious are content living inside their comfort zone, or they are afraid to step outside of it. They lack the desire and vision to grow into someone stronger in the future. They'll criticize you for being "too good for them now" when you start to grow into someone new, and they'll use their victim mentality to trick you into believing that change is a bad thing.

Successful people remove the Envious from their lives, because they lack the vision to see that your success doesn't impede them from doing the same and that your growth should motivate and inspire them to do the same, rather than creating resentment. You'll never win their hearts, because, at the end of the day, their worldview is that success is limited. They're too afraid to go after it, so instead they'll simply hate those who do.

The "Excuse-Makers"

It's the weather's fault I'm late. It's his fault I lost today. It's her fault I'm this way.

The "excuse-makers" are the third type of person you must avoid when building your winning Starting Five. The reason they're not successful is always someone else's fault.

- It's their boss's fault that they haven't grown in their career.

- It's their parents' fault that they continually choose their negative mindset.

- It's their ex's fault that they stay in the same cycle of debt.

It doesn't matter what the reason is; the culprit is never in the mirror for the excuse makers. They lack the ability to take personal responsibility for their own actions in creating their situation. They're entitled, and they believe success is *owed* to them—and if it's not given, then it's someone else's fault.

Carol Dweck profiled one such excuse maker in her book *Mindset: The New Psychology of Success*[12]. She reviewed the career of a famous tennis player in the 1980s. This player was incredibly talented, but he had the bad habit taking all of the credit when he won—and finding an excuse for every reason he lost:

The sun was in my eyes. That fan yelled something to distract me. The ref had it out for me.

It didn't matter if he was simply outplayed. He always had an excuse readily available about who caused him to lose that day—and it was never his own play that was at fault. He was a lightning rod in the sport and was rarely liked.

Compare that with this quotation from Michael Jordan, arguably the greatest basketball player of all time:

> I've missed more than 9,000 shots in my career. I've lost almost 300 games. Twenty-six times I've been trusted to take the game-winning shot and missed. I've failed over and over and over again in my life. And that is why I succeed.[30]

Jordan claimed responsibility for his missed shots and lost games. "I've missed more… I've lost." He wasn't trying to pass the buck onto his teammates, and he wasn't using excuses. He could have easily said he was double-teamed on a shot or that someone in the crowd distracted him. Instead, he owned his shortcomings in those moments.

Those moments are what fueled him to improve and to become the greatest player in his sport's history.

Those that avoid responsibility never see the opportunities to grow.

If nothing is ever your fault when something goes wrong, how can you learn from those experiences and improve? You can't.

Jordan understood the need to take responsibility as a leader—and he used those disappointing setbacks to fuel his growth forward.

Competitors avoid the Excuse Makers, because they know that if you never own up to your shortcomings, you'll never embrace the room to get better.

Three to Look For

Blink three times.

That series of actions—*225 milliseconds*—takes roughly all the time a major league baseball batter has to recognize *and swing* at an incoming pitch. Even less time when it's a fastball over 100 miles per hour. I believe that a major league baseball batter hitting a baseball is the hardest thing to do in sports.

You have to know *exactly* what you're looking for in order to have a chance at making contact with the ball. Great hitters are focused at the plate. Their eyes are locked in on the pitcher: anything that he's doing that can tip off what pitch is coming next and where it will be located.

The batter's eyes will dart from key locations: the pitcher's arm location, wrist angle, release point, and initial spin on the baseball are all key indicators that can help a batter's brain make a decision in the 225 milliseconds they have before the ball gets to the plate.

Batters study pitchers on film, taking notes of every subtle nuance in their delivery, in hopes that it will better prepare them to pick up specific pitches and capitalize on them for a hit on their next at-bat.

In a similar manner, we have to know *exactly* what to look for in healthy relationships in order to build them. Just like a batter dialed into a pitcher's next fastball, we have to lock in on the most important traits of our relationships so that we can succeed with them.

Those Who Inspire Courage

Encouragement is a powerful thing. It's a way to support another, and as researchers have pointed out[1], the goal is "not to change someone's behavior, but to instill the confidence and courage into someone that they can change."[31] The word *encourage* literally means to *inspire courage and strengthen* another. Encouraging other people increases their motivation to take action, rather than forcing them to do so.

"Sticks and stones may break my bones but words will never hurt me." We chant this as kids when people verbally put us down. We tell them that their words can't hurt us, but if we're honest, those words sting. Researchers have shown[2] that the emotional trauma from verbal abuse can have the same impact on our brains as physical abuse[32]. Just because you can't see the scars doesn't mean the effects aren't there.

"The tongue has the power of life and death." (Proverbs 18:21)

Words have the ability to tear down someone's spirit or lift it. If words can create emotional trauma and wound our spirits, then words can also repair that trauma and build up our spirits. Encouragement from our peers can literally change our lives. Just look at the success of peer groups when battling addictions or loss. Countless studies show that these support groups provide community and encouragement for those during their struggles, which ultimately help them overcome their issues.

The person who overcomes does so by finding community and by being encouraged by his or her community.

I gave myself the title of "Chief Encouragement Officer" when I launched Compete Every Day back in 2011. I was inspired by how the *Life Is Good* founders spun their titles to play off of their brand ("Chief Optimism Officer" and "Chief Creative Optimist"), and I wanted a title that would create a conversation—a conversation that, if I played correctly, would provide me the opportunity to encourage everyone with whom I spoke. Before we ever sold our first T-shirt, Compete Every Day's mission was to motivate and encourage Competitors to pursue greatness in every area of their lives.

Just as humans are wired to crave community, our spirits crave encouragement. These special friends are the ones who can speak life into us, lift us up when we've inevitably fallen, and motivate us to keep pressing onward:

- They are the type of teammates who see us struggle and invest extra time after practice to work on what's plaguing us.

- They are the type of mentors who take time out of their busy schedule to text us words of wisdom and encouragement frequently, when we are just starting our careers.

- They are the type of friends who come alongside us during a nasty divorce, encouraging us about what type of person we can be and helping us get back to our feet.

The more we surround ourselves with those who speak life into us, the stronger our lives will be.

Those Who Challenge You

Accountability gets a bad rap. Most people immediately jump to a defensive position when the word comes up in conversation, because it implies that you're going to be judged or criticized for falling short of expectations.

Accountability is one of the truest expressions of love.

Accountability says, "I'm going to hold you to meet the standard that we agreed upon." It's caring enough about someone else's future success that you are willing to call them out when they give poor effort or live in a way that doesn't meet the standard.

It's challenging them by telling them what they *need* to hear instead of only what they want to hear. True friends will stand up to you and speak truth in your life when you're not living up to the person you can be. They'll care more about your future growth than how uncomfortable a conversation may be in the moment.

A friend who challenges you is a friend who cares about you winning.

Those Who Remind You of Who You Want to Be

I'll never forget the look of concern and embarrassment on my roommate's face when he walked in on me back in 2007.

The spring of 2007 was one of my lowest points in life. The girl I'd dated for the previous year had recently cheated on me. I was in the midst of taking graduate school classes for a sports career, even though I was starting to question if it was even still my "dream job." I was also mentally a wreck after believing that I'd let fear negatively influence my athletic career.

I was wracked with regrets, "what-ifs," and a whole lot of inner turmoil. My confidence was shot. My attitude, even more so. I started drinking to cope with my feelings. A small splash here and there throughout the day in a glass of soda turned into a nightly goal of drinking to feel a slight buzz.

Then even more of a buzz.

My breaking point took place on the Wednesday night my roommate came home from his class to find me sitting on our coffee table, playing the Guitar Hero video game, while taking shots from a large bottle of vodka. I'll never forget the look on his face.

He stood in the doorway for a minute, before setting his book bag down and sitting beside me on the coffee table. He looked me right in the eye and said, "I'll play this game with you tonight, but tomorrow we're going to talk about this. Because this is not who you say you want to be."

The next morning, we sat down before work, and we had an honest conversation about how my current actions weren't lining up with the type of person I wanted to be. I posted certain things on social media and told people about my big dreams, but my actions authored a much different story. I was using alcohol to mask my pain, and instead of addressing the issues, I ran from them.

He reminded me that my daily choices were not congruent with the person I said I wanted to be—and that something needed to change. My choices or my goals—I had to choose. He spoke words of encouragement to me and reminded me of who I *could* be with the right changes.

Like most of us, I at first reacted defensively to his words. I wanted to make excuses, but even I knew, deep down, that I was only avoiding the pain instead of proactively building my life.

He cared so much about me that he was willing to have an awkward conversation to encourage me, challenge me, and remind me of who I had the potential to become. It changed my attitude, perspective, and life.

True friends are willing to look you in the eye and see what you're capable of, then to remind you of it whenever you forget. They love you too much to let you settle.

Start in the Mirror

The first thing I do when working with teams on the importance of our relationships to success at work and life is to challenge them to make an exhaustive list of the traits that their *ideal* coworker would have. What do the "perfect" teammates do that would make you want to work alongside them every day?

The list of traits are ones you'd expect people to share:

- being reliable

- having a positive attitude

- being coachable

- being helpful

- taking the initiative

- communicating clearly

- being a consistent worker

Everyone in the audience usually agrees that these traits make up the perfect coworker. Many share that they need someone with all of these traits in order to succeed as a team and organization.

I then ask the room if anyone in the room has every single one of those traits every day at work.

...(insert awkward silence)...

It's easy to carry high expectations for others. Many times, we hold other people to higher standards than we do ourselves. It's like advice—we're always better at giving great advice to others, but we aren't acting on that same advice ourselves.

Before we can build a team of great teammates who encourage us, challenge us, and remind us of who we say we want to be, we first need to become great teammates.

It's not about being perfect but about constantly striving to embody the traits we need others to have. There's no accountability or relationship if one party is held to a different set of rules than the other. Two people unevenly committed to their growth won't last in a relationship long, because eventually the one who's committed to consistently growing will outgrow the relationship with the one who invests in their growth only every now and then.

Competitors focus on improving themselves before they start improving their team. You need to be a growing person in order to attract other growing people. Those leveling up their career, fitness, and life won't shrink themselves down to be at a level below their current state. They'll expect anyone new to rise to their current level—and then push them toward a higher one.

Start Growing

Make a list of the top traits you need in your life's starting lineup. What do your ideal teammates have in common? Write them down.

One good way to create this list is to start reviewing what you want to do in life (professionally, financially, personally) and then align your starting lineup's characteristics with those of the type of people who are succeeding at the goals you've determined.

Want to be financially independent and debt free? Write down the traits of someone you know (or find online) who is financially healthy. What traits—such as being fiscally responsible, valuing experiences over purchases, and the like—does he or she display?

Want to live a healthier lifestyle? What are the traits of those who are mentally and physically healthy? Maybe you are looking for those who practice meditation and meal prep and for those who are goal-oriented and are active daily. Find those people and make the list.

Exhaust your list of the characteristics that embody the type of person that you want to be and the type of people with whom you want to invest time. Start reviewing your list every morning so that those traits become permanent at the forefront of your mind. You'll grow keenly aware of the traits you want to build so that, throughout any given day, when presented with an opportunity or fork in the road, you can choose which action to take *on the basis of the choice that you believe the person you want to become would make.*

The more you start to hone these traits in your life, the more you will start to engage and attract those with similar traits. The more you grow into the type of teammate you want to have in your life, the more opportunities you'll have to connect with growing teammates.

Success requires an investment in ourselves and our friends.

How to Choose Your Teammates

Our friends determine our fate. Be intentional about setting your lineup for life.

Career

1. Make a list of all the traits you want in your ideal coworkers. Start by working on each of those traits yourself.

2. Hiring new talent? Look beyond the résumé. Is the applicant someone who is growth-minded? Does the applicant ask you questions about long-term opportunities and the culture? Ask yourself if this applicant would be a team member who would make your current team members better professionally *and* personally.

3. Find mentors who demonstrate your desired traits. Don't simply ask to be mentored. Ask how you can add value and help them, then start learning from them throughout the process. Consume everything they share online. Ask thoughtful questions. Follow through on the recommendations they make. Show your initiative before you go back asking to learn more. Find the type of professional leaders that you want to emulate and invest time with them.

Health and Fitness

1. Join a group-fitness community. Studio, spin class, yoga, CrossFit, you name it. Find a local place where you can work out and invest time with other people working to be their best selves. Make friends by grabbing coffee after a workout or meeting up before class.

Personal Life

1. Trade one weekend for a leadership-development conference. Invest a few days with like-minded individuals wanting to grow in their skills, careers, mindsets, or lives. Network and connect with these people over your shared growth interests, and start building new friendships.

2. Attend local networking and meetup events. There are thousands of events every day hosted by online networking groups. Research groups that align with your personal interests; then step out of your comfort zone to attend these groups so you can build relationships with other like-minded people.

3. Review your current friendships and the people with whom you spend most of your free time. Do these people fit "What to Find," or do they fit "What to Avoid?" Start investing more time with those who fit the positive attributes, while slowly decreasing your time with those who don't. It's not too late to make new friends. You're not too old. Bury those excuses so that you can build your best life.

4. Be intentional while dating. Don't fall into a trap of choosing people solely on the basis of physical attraction or financial status. Ask yourself if they embody the characteristics you'd want in a long-term teammate. Are they committed to growing? Do they care about your success or just theirs? Be intentional with what can be one of your most important partnerships.

Chapter Takeaways

1. It's convenient to stick with the friendships we "just have," but a winning life requires us to intentionally choose the five people with whom we invest the most time.

2. Our friendships help determine our fate. We can't expect to grow and succeed unless we surround ourselves with other people that are doing the same.

3. Competitors don't take advice from those in the stands. Great athletes understand the importance of focusing on the field and blocking out the fans who aren't playing. The same applies to our lives. Unless other people are willing to compete and take actions in their own lives, their opinions don't count.

4. The "yes men," the envious, and the excuse makers will fill our lives with negativity and drown our chances of success. Just like pruning a flower, we have to cut away toxic and dead relationships so that we can continue to grow.

5. We need relationships that encourage us, challenge us, and remind us of who we say we want to be, in order to continually grow and be sharpened.

6. Before we can expect others to live up to a high standard in their work and workouts and lives, we must first expect ourselves to do so. We set the example in our own lives before we can attract others who are like-minded.

07

Lead with Your Actions

Competitors lead with their lives—not with their lips.

Major league baseball was almost exclusively a white man's sport until the late 1940s. Professional baseball had segregated the MLB leagues from the Negro leagues since the late 1800s. Moses Fleetwood Walker had been the first African American baseball player to play professional minor-league baseball in 1884, but his attempt to break through the racial barriers was quickly thwarted when, in 1889, professional baseball split the leagues into white (MLB) and black (Negro)[33].

Then came 1947.

Jackie Robinson was called up to the Brooklyn Dodgers six days before the 1947 MLB season. A standout athlete while growing up (he was UCLA's first-ever four-sport varsity letterman), Robinson started his baseball career in the Negro Leagues before Brooklyn Dodgers President Branch Rickey signed him to the team's minor-league affiliate. He became the first player to break professional baseball's color line.[34]

His talents on the field were undeniable, and he was quickly moved through the team's minor-league system to its highest professional level, the Dodgers. It was a move that caused uproar throughout the league.

Robinson and his family received death threats from fans. Racial slurs were shouted at him from the stands, from the opposing dugout, and sometimes even from inside his own locker room. Still, Robinson played hard and didn't fight back. He let his play on the field do the talking for him.

Robinson knew that yelling back or getting into a fight wouldn't help him. By letting his actions dictate his response, he would earn the respect of his peers and cement his place on the field. He played hard. He embraced his teammates. He stood strong for something. He didn't just tell others what he believed—he lived it.

Jackie Robinson was inducted into baseball's Hall of Fame in 1962, following a historic career that featured a career batting average of .311 (82nd all-time highest[35]), six All-Star awards, one MVP award, and a World Series championship in 1955. He left the game as one of the best ever.

Even more than how he played the game, he's remembered for his leadership and actions during the sport's most volatile era.

Talk Is Cheap

Any one of us can paint an elaborate story on social media. Almost weekly, an athlete or a celebrity makes up a fictitious story online in order to grab attention—only to be exposed soon after. It's *easy* to talk a big game or to paint a picture that makes you look bigger and better than you actually are.

It's not long before the truth of your actions overshadows your talk or your tweets.

Competitors know that their actions paint the most important pictures of their lives. It's not what we talk about doing that counts, but what we *actually* do. Our actions—not our words—tell our true intentions.

I meant to...

I thought about doing...

I wanted to...

These common excuses run rampant in our culture. Many people fall into the trap of believing that what they *wished* happened should count—instead of what they *actually* did or didn't do. Every single one of us can talk about the things we wish we would accomplish. We can brag about the type of leader we will be one day.

But only the Competitors are keeping their mouths shut while they get to work *actually* achieving the things they want in their careers and lives.

See It; Then Believe It

It's easy for us to hold the perspective that our situation is unique. We can fall into the thinking that the challenges we face are the first of their kind and that no one can relate to what we're going through. Our obstacles are too new, too big, and too scary for anyone to know what we're feeling or facing.

This thinking leads us to believe that we're all alone, in a battle we can't win against our Goliath. We believe it's impossible for us to overcome, and our behaviors shift accordingly.

Our positive attitude starts to diminish. Our actions and efforts slow. Our words? We sound like a defeatist instead of a Competitor. As long as we believe our situation is impossible, we'll behave accordingly and live within those limits.

Run Faster

No human being had ever run a mile faster than four minutes before May 1954. In three thousand years of recorded history, dating back to the ancient Greek Olympics, no one had cracked that mark. The ancient Greeks believed that to run four sixty-second quarters was to run a "perfect race."[1]

Centuries passed, and the dream of running a four-minute mile lived on. In the 1940s, someone ran 4:01. Racers tried to run a 3:59 or faster, but to no avail. Sportswriters around the world even believed it to be physically impossible to run that fast. Their writing led others to believe this, and their opinions became fact in most people's minds.

But on May 6, 1954, a British physician named Roger Bannister ran a 3:59.4 mile, becoming the first person in history to run a mile that fast. As he crossed the finish line and shocked onlookers double-checked their stopwatches, mental and physical barriers around the world fell.

Forty-six days later, someone broke Bannister's mark. As of late 2016, over 4,518 people have run a mile under four minutes, with the current world record set in 1999, a blistering speed of 3:43.13.

It was "impossible" until one person did it. After seeing what could be achieved, others began to follow suit. Their mental limitations fell, as their training intensified. *If Bannister can run a mile under four minutes, so can I,* was their thinking.

His actions inspired them to go after their goals. Other racers removed their self-limiting beliefs and began putting in the work to become someone capable of doing what Bannister did. He proved that what they thought was impossible wasn't.

Slaying That Goliath

Like Bannister's peers, once we see that our impossible situation suddenly isn't, our entire demeanor shifts. We start to believe that if she can overcome this challenge, then "maybe I can too." Our defeatist attitude starts to change as we start to think that we just might have a chance to win.

Our mindset about the challenge changes. Our words turn from those of a victim to those of a potential victor. Our actions follow accordingly, and we start to attack the obstacle like a Competitor instead of just giving up. Here's the biggest key:

Other people are watching you every day.

Whether we realize it or not, every one of us has people who carefully watch our every move. They're studying us to see how we respond to disappointing news. They're wondering how we handle the challenges at work or at home. They're looking to us to lead them through storms.

Once we see someone else doing what we want to do and we're given hope that it's possible to win, we can choose to give our situation our best shot also. The people watching you are inspired by *how you live* and, in turn are motivated to take action, because of what they've seen you do.

You go from being alone in a struggle to being:

- *That woman* who inspired me to keep going when I wanted to quit.

- *That coworker* who gave me the courage to pursue my dream after I watched how he pursued his.

- *That friend* who made me believe in myself when I'd all but given up.

You become their inspiration and difference maker. They realize that their "impossible" situation is a very possible victory, because of how you responded to the same challenge.

It's not because of what you said or what you posted online— but how you lived. It's not your words that will inspire others to change their lives. It's your actions.

Sweep the Parking Lot

I grew up working in a small-town gas station that my dad owned in East Texas. Starting at the age of seven, I'd spend summer days sweeping parking lots, cleaning gas pumps, and stocking the coolers at the store. These were my chores before I could play with my neighborhood friends or head to baseball practice.

I hated every minute of it.

Sometimes my dad would jump in and help me stock the cooler or change out a soda line that had run out of syrup. I didn't understand why he would do that or why he was making me work in the store. "Didn't we pay employees to do all of this?" I asked him one day.

"We do—but many times throughout life, a leader has to get in there and do the work himself."

He went on to teach me about the importance of setting the example for a team. He said, "It doesn't matter how high up you are in the company, how much money you make, or what your title is—a great leader will always set the example with his life instead of just his lips. Great leaders are never too high and mighty to roll up their sleeves and sweep the parking lot, if that's what it takes to help the team succeed.

"Besides, if I'm going to ask my team to do a task, I need to show them that I'm willing to do it, too. Nothing is beneath me or them."

Sweep Up the Sugar

Just because you make more money than others in a company doesn't make you a more important human than they are. Competitors make great leaders because they're willing to put in the work that they also expect others to perform.

Compare my dad's work ethic with that of an individual that I worked with years later as a consultant. This particular individual had experienced some success decades earlier and still mentally lived in that era. He was in a position of authority as owner of an organization, but he would never even make his own cup of tea. He'd make a mess at the conference table during meetings with sugar packets and spilled tea, but he would never clean it up— always leaving it for someone on his team to pick up after him.

Even worse, 99 percent of the time that *someone* that he asked to clean up after him was a female employee.

He expected high standards and accountability in his employees, but he failed to lead in a similar manner. He saw himself as better than his employees; then he wondered why his company culture became toxic.

Culture starts at the top. Leadership is influenced by actions, not words on a wall or printed in a mission statement.

Sweep the Sheds

The New Zealand All Blacks are one of the most feared rugby teams in the sport's history, and one of the most dominant franchises of all time. They have a franchise lifetime winning percentage of 77 percent, higher than any other team in any other sport in the world.

As documented in James Kerr's book *Legacy: What the All Blacks Can Teach Us About the Business of Life*, one thing that sets the All Blacks apart from other teams is their culture of "sweeping the shed." It is the tradition that no individual player is bigger than the team and its history. Everyone is responsible for every single detail, including "sweeping the shed" (cleaning out the locker room after a match). Before leaving the dressing room after a match, players tidy up after themselves, leaving the room spotless. It doesn't matter if you're the biggest star in the sport or a rookie, all members of the team take responsibility to pick up after themselves.

This culture of personal responsibility and leadership has helped continue their culture of dominance on the field by making sure every player is committed to one truth: no one is too big to do the little things and to do them well.

Managers Manage; Leaders Lead

There's a difference between having a title and being a leader. Titles go on business cards, professional résumés, and organizational charts. But they have little to do with being a leader, other than that the expectation that the more prestigious your title, the better leader you should be.

Managers have a fancy title, higher pay, and *tell* their teams what to do. They rely on their mouths and care little if their own actions go against the standard that they have set for others. Managers don't do the dirty work, because, as I heard someone say in an office, "I pay someone to do that type of work. That's beneath my time."

Leaders come in all shapes and sizes, and they influence their teams on actions and success—while setting the example themselves by how they act. Leaders pay teammates to do specific roles but aren't afraid to step in and help if a need arises. Be it in a presentation, cleaning the office kitchen sink, or carrying boxes into a new office.

A leader is never too big to roll up her sleeves and do the dirty work.

Let Them Do It

"It's not my job; let someone else do it."

Nothing irritates me more than seeing abandoned shopping carts littered across a parking lot. I counted a total of ten carts between my two stops in a retail center the day I wrote this. The sign of carts left scattered in the wild screams *"entitlement."* More than anything, it shows a lack of personal responsibility.

You see the same type of behavior when someone

- Refuses to rack their weights in the gym
- Pees all over the toilet seat and then doesn't clean it up
- Tosses litter out of his or her car window on the highway

It's all an attempt to pass the buck to someone else. The attitude of "it's not my responsibility; let someone else deal with it" isn't one of a leader.

Or anyone of success, for that matter.

People moan about the government, even though they haven't voted in a decade. Those same people complain they're getting passed over for a promotion at work, even though they've barely put forth the effort to enhance their career skills.

Those same people are the ones most likely to whine that they aren't as fit as that other person in the gym, even though they're eating junk food daily and working out only once a week, while that other person is following a meal plan daily and training multiple times a week.

It's always "someone else's fault" that some people aren't receiving the successes they believe they're owed, instead of taking responsibility for their own actions that put them in that losing position in the first place.

- Tired of being in debt? Quit spending frivolously. Make a plan that you can follow daily to earn more and to spend less.

- Tired of sucking at a certain movement in the gym? Hire a coach to help you work on that specific movement and on complementary accessory work.

- Tired of going to a job you abhor? Invest thirty minutes every morning before work or every night after work to learn new skills that you can use to transfer positions or change companies.

One can't embrace a martyr's mindset and a Competitor's mindset simultaneously. You have to choose one or the other.

You get to choose to be the hero or the victim, but never both. If you're choosing to be a Competitor, then it's your responsibility to save yourself, instead of waiting for someone else to save you.

You can't be a Competitor if you're going to shirk responsibility. The three things we always control are

- Our focus

- Our attitude

- Our actions

So it's 100 percent on us if we *choose* to pass the blame to someone else or to take responsibility for our actions. It's also 100 percent on us if we're going to choose to lead others by showing them how to take responsibility.

It's on Me

Michael Jordan was sitting at the back of his Chicago Bulls team bus in tears. It was June 1990, and Jordan's Bulls had just been knocked out of the playoffs for the third straight year by Detroit's "Bad Boy" Pistons.[14] The NBA all-star was overcome with anger and sadness at yet another disappointing series loss to their Eastern Conference rivals. As he shared with Tony Robbins, he was preparing to erupt at his teammates about their poor play. He was tired of losing to Detroit, and it was his teammates' fault they hadn't won.

In that moment, he was hit with the realization that his current emotional state wasn't going to change the situation. Crying about the loss wouldn't help him win next year. Yelling at his teammates and blaming them wasn't going to build a team capable of getting over their playoff hurdle.

Jordan said that in that moment, he realized *he had to be better.*

It was in that subsequent off-season that he poured himself into the weight room, forging himself into a bigger, stronger player. The following season, the Jordan-led Bulls toppled the Pistons on their way to their first of three straight championships.

Jordan discovered that the change he desired began with him. It wasn't on his teammates to elevate their play—it was on him. If he wanted to have a better team, he had to start by being a better player. His decision to take personal responsibility for every aspect of his play and team led him to becoming the greatest basketball player of all time.

Look in the Mirror

It's easy for us to look to others to change our situation. It's more convenient if someone else could come in and make the necessary changes for us.

Leadership doesn't start with someone else. It starts with us.

Earlier we discussed the importance of avoiding excuse makers in order to create a thriving career and life. A big reason for this avoidance is that excuse makers lack personal responsibility. They are quick to claim credit when things go their way, but when they don't?

It's never *their* fault. They fail to see any fault in their own actions and efforts. This creates a false reality in their mind; because they believe in their own perfection, they therefore fail to see room for growth.

If you think that everything you do is great, then why would you ever find opportunities to improve?

Competitors aren't lulled into thinking they're blameless. Just as Jordan discovered that it was on him as a leader to set the tone and raise his game, it's on you to step it up a level in your office and in your home. If you want others to do the same, you need to take responsibility for every area of your work and life and to identify ways you can be a better contributor—helping others, too.

Taking responsibility is the way for leaders to seize the opportunity to solve their own problems. It's understanding that not everything happening is their fault; rather, it's believing that it's on them as leaders to try to help improve the situation.

Is it traffic's fault that you're late to a meeting, or did you fail to take proper consideration of how long it may take to get there?

Is it the boss's fault you weren't promoted, or is there room for you to improve your work so that there's no question you're the most valuable employee in your division?

Is it your teammate's fault you lost this week's game, or were there plays in the first half where you could have performed stronger, had you been better prepared?

Competitors know their work starts in the mirror first. Always see it as *your* responsibility.

Game Time Adjustments

The halftime score of Super Bowl LI was 21–3 in favor of the Atlanta Falcons. It looked as if the Dirty Birds would win their first championship in franchise history, especially after they scored another touchdown to start the third quarter and took a commanding 28–3 lead.

Football games aren't won after thirty-six minutes. They're won after sixty.

The New England Patriots went on to score thirty-one unanswered points and to win the largest comeback in NFL history, 34–28 in overtime. How did they do it?

By making the right game-time adjustments.

Good coaches have a strong game plan heading into a game. Great coaches are those who can make the winning adjustments at halftime. They can see what an opponent has done well and where their own team has struggled, and they can make adjustments on the fly to overcome those challenges.

A winning Competitor has to do the same.

Life is going to challenge you. It's going to throw curveballs at you and knock you off balance. Winning requires your ability to adjust to the things that you don't see coming.

A Competitor chooses to make adjustments over excuses. It doesn't matter what your career or life is throwing at you—what matters is how you respond to it.

Any of us can create an excuse at any given second. It's easier than actually doing the work required. Excuses don't change our situation, and they've never gotten the job done.

Excuses don't cash checks. Excuses aren't what people brag about. Excuses will always be available—but opportunities won't be.

Most people around you use their favorite excuses. All of the time. For everything.

They always have a reason why they aren't winning. They blame the weather, their parents, their boss, or their mood. There's always someone or something to blame for their lack of success.

Except for their own actions and efforts.

Competitors kill their excuses. They don't complain or whine if they lose; they simply learn from that situation and make adjustments for their next opportunity.

Bad weather caused problems during my first trip. What adjustments in my preparation can I make before I go out of town next time?

My boss said that my numbers weren't strong enough for a promotion. What adjustments can I make in my daily process to raise those numbers?

My last three relationships have failed for the same reasons. What adjustments can I make in *how I date* and in the type of people I *intentionally* look for before I meet someone else?

Notice what wasn't just listed? Excuses.

Your success in anything—working out, starting a business, playing sports, dating, raising a family, and the like—comes down to your ability to make adjustments in your own actions, instead of relying on excuses.

How to Lead Better

Talk is cheap. Our actions and lives paint the loudest picture of what it means to be a Competitor.

Career

1. Never let your title or your paycheck trick you into believing you're "above it." Set the example for your coworkers and team by doing great work—even the dirty work that someone else may be paid to do. Before you ask others in your office to do something for you, make sure they know you'd do it yourself.

2. Own your mistakes. When you mess up, own it to your team. Don't blame others; don't make excuses. Take full responsibility for the error, and let them know what you'll do to be better the next time.

Health and Fitness

1. Never cheat reps. If a workout calls for "x" number of rounds or reps, do them all. It doesn't matter if you finish last; never cheat reps. Set the example for other members that your placement in a daily workout doesn't matter but that your commitment to getting better does.

2. Rack your weights. Clean up after yourself. Maybe even be the type of leader who helps others to pick up their weights and clean down the station. Always take responsibility for what you've taken out and done.

Personal Life

1. Accept the challenge of today. Others are watching us every day, so instead of complaining about a negative situation you find yourself in, choose a positive attitude and attack it.

2. Kill off your excuses. Commit to yourself that you're better than your excuses. Leaders take responsibility for all of their actions.

3. Rack your shopping cart. Wipe down the airport sink if you made a mess. Be a Competitor who takes responsibility for picking up after himself, whether there is someone else paid to do the work or not.

4. Make sure your hustle says more than your mouth. It's easy to talk about everything you're going to do one day. Most people who talk nonstop about their big future achievements never take the action to reach them. Your walk speaks louder than your talk, so walk in the reality that what you say is less important than what you choose to do with your actions.

Chapter Takeaways

1. No one is inspired by how big we talk. They're inspired by how big we live.

2. A Competitor's life inspires others by showing the limits that others just accept as "impossible" to overcome aren't "impossible."

3. Leaders set the example in how they do the smallest of tasks. You're never too big to sweep the parking lot or to clean the sink, because it shows your teammates that no one is above the team.

4. Competitors take personal responsibility for their actions. Someone else isn't coming to save you—you have to be the one who saves yourself.

5. Competitors make adjustments, not excuses, when life throws them challenges. Own your actions, your effort, and your attitude, and make the most of every day.

08

Always Do Your Best

It doesn't matter how you feel—it matters what you do.

Life is full of things we don't control: The weather, where we are born, our boss's attitude. Pick something, and despite your best attempts, chances are it's outside of your control.

Too many people waste the limited resources of their time and energy trying to change what's outside of their control. They fixate their focus on what's happening in someone else's lane. They allow others' actions to dictate their own attitudes. They fluctuate their efforts on the basis of situations beyond their control.

They end up losing in the big picture because of it, and they always wonder why.

What's outside your control doesn't matter. What you do control does, because it's the only thing you can influence.

Attitude. Effort. Actions.

The only things we control in life are our attitudes, our efforts, and our actions. Nothing else.

We don't control our spouses. We don't control our natural talents. We don't control the weather.

But we always control how we *choose* to respond to those things.

The darkest period of my professional career happened five years after I started my first company. Our industry shifted, and I was off target in estimating the time when we needed to make certain changes. I had to cut certain contracts. I skipped my paycheck more than once to make sure the team members that I had left were still paid. I stared as my debts rose while our sales started to decline.

I battled anxiety and dark thoughts on a daily basis. I saw no way out, and it was easy to find reasons to blame our situation on other things. I could easily rattle off three or four reasons that we were in the shape that we were. I saw no way out of the hole I'd dug us into.

One morning, I was watching TV, and an athlete was being interviewed after a huge comeback win. His team had been down a few touchdowns, and when reporters asked him how his team had won the game, he told them, "We just kept believing we could and focused only on the next play."

For some reason, that line stuck with me: "Focus only on the next play." In sports, the only play you control is the *next* one. You control what attitude you will *choose* going into that play. You also control what effort you'll *choose* to give and what actions you'll *choose* to take.

You can't control the next series or even the next quarter—but you can put yourself in a better position by taking care of business on this next play. That day, I stopped stressing about the entire mountain of debt I had or everything that needed to change in our company. I instead focused on what we were going to do today.

It seems overwhelming to dig yourself out of a mile-deep ditch with a hand shovel, but you can do it, if you quit staring at how far you have left to dig and just start digging.

I told myself that I was going to smile through the stress and to focus on what I controlled—effort, attitude, and actions—every day until we got out of that hole. I started small by down-loading some introductory podcast episodes on budgeting for business. I created a new spreadsheet to track every single penny that came into the company, and then I created columns that would automatically calculate the percentages I needed to invest into operations, marketing, and paying off the debt.

I spent time in that spreadsheet every day, reviewing cash flow and testing which columns I could modify in order to pay down the debt at a faster rate. I started small (10 percent) and gradually grew.

It wasn't easy.

Many days, it was hard to smile while I was digging, but day after day, I did my best until I looked up one day and realized we were out of debt.

I didn't dig myself out on day one, but the key is that I started digging. People can't change their situations without taking action, even if it's only a fraction of a step forward.

It doesn't matter if you brought on your circumstances your-self or if they were brought on by things outside of your control. What matters is whether or not you choose to do your best in those circumstances to *grow* out of them. Our attitude, efforts, and actions in each situation, good or bad, come down to what choices we make in that moment. Will we let how we feel or where we are dictate control of what we control—or will we refuse to give that power to anyone but ourselves?

We control whether or not we're going to let our spouses' bad days at work be the reasons we get angry at them at night.

We control whether or not we're going to let our lack of a certain natural talent level be the reason we give subpar effort at work.

Yes, we even control whether or not we're going to let the weather dictate if we're going to get up and go to the gym before work.

It's easy to give up our power over the three things we do control to influences beyond our control. That would be making excuses, right? We've already determined that Competitors make adjustments instead of excuses. Adjusting means changing the plan while maintaining control of what you control, but excuses try to deflect responsibility for your own choices from the equation.

In order to win our work, workouts, and lives, we have to be people who always maintain control of our attitudes, efforts, and actions. It doesn't matter what our circumstances are or what someone else does. It matters what we do.

The key to winning at life is to make sure that what's outside of your control does not control your ability to do your best with what is in your control.

Does Your Position Influence Your Output?

I went into my junior year of varsity football fully expecting to ride the bench. The senior ahead of me was talented and firmly cemented as the starter heading into the new season. I knew I'd get one series per game for experience and preparation in the rare instance I was needed.

I remember sitting outside of my locker on the Friday morning of our first game, when our running backs coach came over and took a seat next to me. Coach Gideon handed me a small devotional book and encouraged me to give it a read. Then, as he got up, he turned and said:

You don't have to stress about being ready to play if you're always ready.

I shrugged off the words, knowing better, and knowing that I wouldn't be playing, but I felt obligated to read the book. It talked about the importance of being ready and giving your best efforts, regardless of whether you were the starter, the back up, or the fifth stringer. Winners don't stress about having to get ready when an opportunity arrives, because they are constantly training with the intention of playing. They give 100 percent effort, no matter where they are on the depth chart, knowing that if they do, they'll be ready to seize the moment if they're needed on the field.

Unbeknownst to me, my moment would arrive two weeks later in the third game, when our starter went down with an injury.

Have you ever seen a deer in headlights? I imagine that's what I looked like to the opposing linebackers. As a predator would say, I was *fresh meat*. We ended up winning a close game, but I made numerous mistakes, including throwing an interception and missing some wide-open passes.

I wasn't ready for the moment, because I hadn't planned to be in the moment. I'd let my position on the depth chart influence my preparation. If I'd wanted to excel when my moment came, I had to be relentlessly preparing, as if the opportunity would be there any second. Fortunately, that one game taught me a lesson that I have never forgotten. Even though I went back to being the backup the next week, I was religious about preparing for every game. I studied films, practiced harder, and waited on the sideline, ready. If I was needed, I planned to grab the moment.

Later that season, I was called on again. I led our team to one of the best playoff runs in school history. This happened only after more weeks of playing the backup—but I was preparing as if I were the starter.

Compare my lack of preparation with that of Nick Foles, the backup who was a Super Bowl MVP.

Multiple times during his NFL career, Foles went into the season as a backup, only to be thrust into the starting position when the starting quarterback was injured. In week fourteen of the 2017 season, Foles stepped in for an injured Carson Wentz and led the Philadelphia Eagles to their first Super Bowl title in team history while earning MVP honors in the game. The following season, he led the team to multiple wins and the playoffs while again filling in for the injured Wentz.

Foles signed an $88 million contract in the off-season because of his play coming off the bench.[36] Even with a great team around him, he wouldn't have won a Super Bowl MVP, multiple NFL games, or cashed in that massive contract, unless he was constantly preparing to start while still a backup.

Frank Reich spent most of his NFL career as a backup to Hall of Famer Jim Kelly, but Reich is famous for stepping in to win two of the biggest comebacks in football history. His first happened in college, when he filled in and rallied Maryland from a 31–0 deficit to beat the University of Miami. His second? Helping the Buffalo Bills rally to beat the Houston Oilers in a game known in NFL history as "the Comeback." He has a quotation in his office:

> There's a certain sense of spontaneity a backup quarterback must accept: You toil in the shadows until you're suddenly asked to become a savior. You don't know when it will come, if it will come.[37]

Reich wouldn't be known in college football and professional football history if he hadn't been prepared when his opportunities suddenly arrived. He'd be forgotten in football lore with the dozens of backups who, when thrust into a game unexpectedly, struggled because they hadn't ever prepared to play.

Your preparation and effort shouldn't be influenced by the place where you are on the depth chart on your team, on your office organizational chart, or in your life right now. If it is, how can you expect to be ready when an opportunity suddenly appears?

Leaders don't stress about being ready for the moment when it arrives, because they've been slowly putting in the work for that moment. They anticipate it. They welcome it.

Most of all, they're prepared to seize it because of what they've done long before that moment showed up.

Wins Don't Carry Over

Babe Ruth is famous for saying, "Yesterday's home runs don't count for today's games." We can't bring the hits from the past into the present and expect them to count.

Just as great backups have to be ready before their moments arrive, some people already in the spotlight can't let their feet off the gas. Time after time, we see some people work hard, get to the top, and then quickly fall back down because they started resting on their past successes.

How often are some people promoted to manager or assigned that fancy corner office, only to see their production slip and their attitude change? They went from being driven to grow their careers to being comfortable while taking it easy in their new roles.

Winning back-to-back championships is one of the hardest accomplishments in sports for two reasons: 1) every team starts aiming for you once they know you're the champ, but even more important, 2) it's hard to stay motivated and to keep giving your best efforts in training and performance after you've already won. Players relax and decrease their effort after having already been to the peak in their sport.

It's hard to reach the top. It's even harder to stay there.

Legendary Competitors keep their foot on the gas to win multiple championships. They remain as hungry for their third championship as they did for their first. They believe in training their hardest and in giving their best effort in the final week of the season as they gave in the first.

One of the most impressive athletic feats I've had the pleasure of watching was the four-peat CrossFit Games championships by Rich Froning and Mathew Fraser, as well as the three-peat by Tia-Clair Toomey. These individuals train essentially year-round and are able to remain hungry mentally, still driven to succeed even after winning the championship one, two, and three times! It's hard enough to stay motivated after your first victory, much less a third straight victory.

Their situation—having won before—doesn't change their training and output. If anything, it helps them take it up a level, knowing that others are gunning for their top spot.

Competitors don't allow their current position to influence their output. They always give their best, regardless of where they are.

No Shoes? Doesn't Matter

Jim Thorpe, arguably the greatest athlete ever, represented the United States in track and field during the 1912 Olympics. He dominated the first five events, placing first in four of them. His next event, a three-day decathlon, is where things got interesting.

Thorpe crushed the field in a pouring rain for his first event, the 100-meter dash, with a time of 11.2 seconds that stayed an Olympic record for thirty-six more years. As Thorpe went out on the second day, he found his shoes were missing. Someone had taken them. Choosing not to let that stop him, Thorpe wore a pair of mismatched shoes[38]—one borrowed from a teammate and another found in a nearby trashcan—to compete in the high jump (which he won). One of the mismatched shoes was even too big, which forced Thorpe to wear extra socks in order to tighten its fit.

Despite wearing two mismatched shoes that weren't even his own, Thorpe gave his best and competed in the remaining decathlon events, winning multiple competitions and eventually a gold medal for the event.

Do you care about making excuses or showing up and doing your best?

So what if they stole your shoes? Find another pair and compete as hard as you can.

So what if your job sucks? Work on building skills to go earn a new one.

So what if the weather is bad? Get out of bed like you said you would and compete in the gym.

The simple fact is this: excuses don't create champions, and champions don't create excuses. You have the choice every day to make excuses about why you didn't give your best effort, why you chose a bad attitude, or why you failed to take action. You also have the choice to instead do your absolute best with what you control in every situation.

But you can't do both.

What's Easy?

It's easy to let our current circumstances and feelings influence our actions. But Competitors show up with their full effort every time, especially when they don't feel motivated.

It's easy to go half-speed and cheat yourself during today's workout, because you know that someone else in the class is better at the movements than you are. But Competitors don't let what someone else is doing distract them from doing their best work to improve their skills today.

It's easy to slack off when you take an unpaid internship and there's no money coming in for your efforts. A Competitor shows up every day, ready to help the team.

It's easy to have a poor attitude when you have to take a job that's below your skill level and experience. Competitors show up and do their best work wherever they are—because it's the only way that will one day get them to where they want to be.

Who Cares If No One Sees?

Doing your best requires a level of accountability with yourself to do what's required—even if no one else is watching.

Although I actively carve out time four to five times a week to lift weights, I used to hate lifting. Especially squats. I wasn't the most flexible of athletes, and I hated heavy back squats. Since it's one of the best lifts for building strength, it was one I was stuck doing throughout my sports career.

I'll never forget one particular weight-room session during my freshman year of high school. We were in the middle of a lower-body lifting session during off-season training. My partner and I were trading out sets of different exercises when it came time for the back-squat station. Neither of us really wanted to do all three sets of ten reps, so we made a deal to (quietly) do just two sets of the exercise. We'd take our time and rotate slower than normal so that we were able to stay busy for the entire time allotted to that station.

The coach's whistle blew, signaling it was time to change stations, so the two of us racked the weight and started heading over to the next station. Our coach then blew a second whistle and yelled for everyone to take a knee.

He then turned, and, with eyes that bore holes into my soul, he asked if my partner and I had done all three sets of our squats.

It was one of those moments we've all had with a parent or a person of authority. We've done something that we know we shouldn't have and are then asked about it. We *know deep down* that they know the truth, and they are giving us two options: come clean and admit that we messed up, or lie and dig our grave deeper.

We looked at each other, and, without saying a word, we agreed that lying would only make things worse. We confessed to skipping reps.

To say we were scolded would be an understatement. My coach ripped us apart in front of the team. Everyone on the team was forced to do pushups because of our laziness in the moment, and then my partner and I were sent outside to run hill sprints. I could've been angry in that moment, but it was no one's fault but our own. We failed to hold ourselves accountable, and we were forced to "pay up" for our lapse in judgement.

I'll never forget my coach talking to us after what felt like 100 hill sprints. He said, "Jake, if you're not going to be accountable to yourself to do your best when no one is watching, then how are your teammates in the locker room going to rely on you? If you can't show up with 100 percent effort on things that you don't necessarily want to do, do you think you can lead others to do so? You have to be a leader who does what's right, and needed, regardless of whether a coach is watching or you want to be doing it."

Competitors understand that to be leaders others can rely on, they must have the discipline to hold themselves accountable, as well as to show up and do their best even when they don't want to be there.

The easy route is letting your attitude and effort dip to the level of your current circumstances.

Don't want to do that workout? Coast through the movements, or, as we did, cut your reps short as an excuse.

Don't like your boss? Give half effort at work, knowing that you don't care if he gets mad at you.

Don't like your current teammates? Avoid confrontation, let them get away with poor effort, and fail to hold them accountable.

This is the path most people take, believing they can simply "flip a switch" when an opportunity arrives, and they'll be able to seize it. Life doesn't work that way. You sacrifice what's most important later when you give into your feelings in the moment.

Your opportunity is coming, whether you're ready for it or not. It's only by preparing for it before it ever comes into view that you're able to seize it. If you try to prepare for the moment when it arrives, it'll slip from your grasp, as if you were trying to hold water in your hand.

You prepare for the inevitable opportunity by showing up every day, embracing the process, and doing your best in the moment. You prepare for your inevitable win by not letting your current feelings, position, or circumstances keep you from doing the necessary work to get better.

Our feelings aren't facts, and our current circumstances don't have to be permanent. The only way we change them is by taking action today, regardless of whether or not we feel motivated.

There are a number of things in this life that we don't control: the weather, our boss, our teammates, politics, and the like. They will always exist, and it's easy to let them distract us from what we do control.

Our focus. Our effort. Our choices.

We control 100 percent of what we choose to focus on.

We control 100 percent of the actions we take to move forward.

We control 100 percent of the choices when we choose to give 10 percent or 100 percent effort.

We control that. Us. Nothing else.

It's easy to let the things outside of our control influence what is, but that's not how a Competitor chooses to operate.

One Percent Difference

I do not consider myself a morning person. At all.

In high school and college, I would sleep until noon if I could. I love to sleep. When I wanted to get back into shape in my twenties, I started going to the gym in the morning before work. The first week sucked.

My alarm would go off at five o'clock in the morning. I'd sleepwalk to put my gym clothes on, and I'd head out the door. Without a jolt from a caffeinated pre-workout drink, I might have fallen asleep on a bench press. ("Um, excuse me sir, are you using these weights or napping?")

Eventually, my body adjusted to the early mornings, and waking up at five became easier. I was up and ready to go, often without needing the caffeine boost to wake up. I didn't start that way.

Years later, as a newly married man, I learned that my wife is anything but a morning person and that our two dogs will bark and stir at the softest of sounds. Just as I had developed a strong morning routine, my habits began to change, and that small choice to start my day before the sun came up slowly morphed into sleeping until seven in the morning, when she would get up.

I would justify sleeping two hours later with the excuse that I "didn't want to wake her or the dogs." But, in reality, I enjoyed my sleep and had made small 1 percent choices that had added up to break the morning routine I had once built. I needed to start over.

I started by setting my alarm at 6:30 a.m. for a week to ease back into the early mornings. Then 6:00 a.m. a week later, and then 5:30 a.m., consistently. I still feel the temptation of my snooze alarm, and I won't lie: I have hit it. I never hit it two days in a row.

Small choices, when compounded day after day, add up to help or to hurt our progress. The easiest way to stop a downward spin?

Never Have Two Bad Days in a Row.

All of us who have declared we are going "lose weight and get healthy" have stumbled. Pizza, beer, wine—it knows us by name and calls out in the sweetest of voices. We slip and gorge out on the cheat meal of choice.

This is the tipping point to failure for most people. The one bad meal becomes two, and then three, and when you look up two weeks later, you've binged on everything you'd given up the previous month, so you decide to quit your health goals.

We mess up once and then make excuses to justify the next lapse in judgement because of the previous one. Our best way to fight back? Make the choice that you won't start a losing streak. Cut the error at one.

You had a meal that wasn't on your training plan? It's okay. Make the next meal great.

You missed a day at the gym? Don't miss tomorrow.

You screwed up a relationship? Learn from your mistakes and make the next one better.

Every Choice Matters.

It's easy to justify one bad choice with another. We rationalize that small choices aren't "that big of a deal." In the moment, they may not be. When done repeatedly, they become a very big deal.

If you made one bad choice, then make the next one a good one. Start a winning streak, instead of submitting to a losing one. Apply the midnight rule to your moment and focus on what's next.

The small choices that are unnoticeable on the surface are the ones that create very noticeable changes when you add them up over time.

Competitors know that the details that most think don't matter are often the ones that do.

Raise Your Baseline

One thing that I have always loved about weightlifting is that it's a continual pursuit of *more*. We follow training programs in order to become more efficient at certain movements and stronger at specific lifts. Each training session is a chance to boost our ability to a new level.

Like most training programs, our maximum weight lifted starts to increase throughout the program. Say I want to start a new squat program. I will max out my strength at squatting the week before I start the new training program so that I know my current ceiling. I then use percentages of that maximum squat weight as guidelines for the six-, eight-, or twelve-week training program.

At the end of the program, I max out again, having increased my total weight lifted anywhere from five to fifteen pounds.

If I were to start a new program, I'd then calculate new percentages on the basis of my new squat personal record. My baseline was raised to a new high. It would be silly to use my original percentages in a new program, because I'm stronger now.

My threshold has grown, and with it, what's possible to lift has also grown. I raise the bar and my baseline on my strength by stepping outside of comfort zone, following a training program to its full extent and pushing myself.

It's funny how life works the same way.

Each time we lean into that discomfort, we increase our comfort dealing with discomfort. It's never "easy," but we grow more accustomed to the feelings of discomfort and less likely to run from them. Like lifters who continue to gain strength and to raise their baseline weight, we continually grow in our careers, our relationships, and our lives, raising our baseline of what's deemed "possible."

What we accepted as quality work as a freshman in high school is quite different than what we should accept as quality work as a senior in college. Our skills have matured, our knowledge has deepened, and we have more experience. Our quality should increase over time so that what passed for us at age fourteen isn't remotely close to what we should strive for a baseline at age twenty-two.

The only way we grow our baseline is by doing our best and then immediately planning how to beat it. I won't get much (if any) stronger doing a squat program just on the days I feel like it. I won't get much out of a lifting session if I scale down the weights dramatically because I don't want to lift heavy that day, despite my program calling for lifting heavy. My comfort zone will practically kill my chances for growth.

Similarly, we fail to grow in our lives if we only accept easy challenges. Living complacently within our comfort zone robs us of the opportunity to grow, because it keeps our baseline at a level well within our reach. We don't grow. We don't increase our skills. Ten years from now, we end up being at the exact same level as we are now. Talk about a wasted decade.

Showing up and doing your best at the gym when you don't feel motivated to work out increases your tolerance to show up and to do your best at work, when you don't like your job.

Giving 100 percent effort to prepare and present that public speaking opportunity that you're terrified of better equips you to walk across the bar and to ask out that attractive person you don't know.

Picking up the phone to make sales calls after repeatedly hearing "no" builds the resilience you need when life repeatedly tries to deal you challenges.

The struggle—and our leaning into the struggle by consistently giving our full effort—is what increases our threshold and raises the baseline of what we accept as our standard. The higher our standard goes, the better our output at work, in the gym, and in life. The better our quality of output grows, the bigger our success grows.

Standards aren't raised by playing it safe or small.

How to Always Do Your Best

A key to winning at life is to do your best with what you control every day, while not letting what you don't control derail you.

Career

1. Do your best work, every day, no matter if it's an internship, a position you hate, or the dream job you love. Be reliable and on time, and do your best work every opportunity you get.

2. Find your competitive advantage and double down on it. Don't let what others may or may not have keep you from doing great work. Is a rival company better funded than your team? Doesn't matter. Does that other company have longer history in the industry? Doesn't matter. Does that employee have a more prestigious education? Doesn't matter. What matters is what work you will do to find your advantage and to build on it.

3. Be the coworker who always chooses a positive attitude and who does his or her best work. From the trivial projects to the make-or-break ones, be the employee and leader your team knows that will always bring his or her "A" game to every situation.

Health and Fitness

1. Don't let the weather, the snooze alarm, or your current motivation levels determine if you follow through with your commitment to eat well or work out today. Do let your long-term goals determine if you do.

2. Focus on compounding today's efforts with yesterday's. Remember the 1 percent growth? Build on it. Don't be distracted by how far you have left to go or by how much work is still required to reach your goal—simply ask how you can build on yesterday. Then take action at the dinner table and on the training platform.

3. Challenge yourself to raise your baseline—especially on the days you don't feel like doing your best. Raise the minimum acceptable effort from what it was yesterday to a new level today. Push yourself. Lean into the discomfort. Rest assured afterwards, knowing you got better.

Personal Life

1. Show up with a positive attitude and outlook in every situation. Choose to shine in the situations you want to be in and in the ones you don't. Be consistent in your choices. Anyone can make excuses when they don't want to be "there." You can't tell Competitors that they don't want to be there, because they've chosen to have a great attitude, while doing great work.

2. Raise your acceptable minimum effort every week. Don't allow yourself to sink to last year's level or last decade's benchmark. Do better today.

Chapter Takeaways

1. No matter what, you always control your attitude, your effort, and your actions. Blaming someone else when you falter with these three is simply an excuse and a lack of personal responsibility. Own what you control, and do your best every day.

2. Success comes down to being able to maintain power and focus on what we control, instead of letting the things we don't distract us.

3. In order to reach the opportunities they want to have, Competitors do their best with the opportunities they're not excited about.

4. Excuses will never save the day for you. Show up with a positive attitude and your best efforts every day, no matter

how you feel, how the weather is, or what someone else does. Your success comes down to owning your actions, your efforts, and your attitudes consistently over time.

5. Consistent effort over time will take your "can't see" choices in the moment that seem inconsequential and create "can't miss" results over time. Focus on how you show up today, and the results of tomorrow will take care of themselves.

6. Your goal every day should be to raise your baseline and the minimum possible standard. Growth and success come from continuing to level up in our endeavors.

09

Help Others Win, Too

Leadership isn't about your social media following.

I grew up in a family of teachers. My mom has been an elementary school teacher throughout my life. My grandmother (on my paternal side) taught elementary school for decades before retiring (and subsequently returning as an occasional substitute). My dad's brother and his wife both teach high school students. Books were put in my hand, and activities were taught to me from a young age.

I had no chance to escape learning.

One thing that I have appreciated about teachers more, as I've aged, is how their work literally changes lives—but how they aren't looking for the credit.

My mom has won teacher of the year twice for her school, yet when asked, each time she deflects the attention and puts it back on her team of coteachers and the students. She doesn't care about awards; she only cares that the students enjoy learning.

Their long-term success is more important than any short-term award she receives.

All great teachers and coaches share this thinking. It's not about them but about the people they're investing in so they can succeed. If they can teach you a subject, a strategy, or a way to succeed and if you succeed at it, that's more important to them than getting credit for teaching it to you. Your success as a student matters more to them than their accolades as teachers.

Great leadership works the same way.

Social media can trick us into believing that our leadership ability is determined by the number of followers that we have on any given platform. The greater the leader, the more followers they have, online and offline. Just like great teachers, great leaders invest in their following to help them up to their own level as leaders. True leaders don't want to lead by themselves; they want to help create other leaders to stand beside them.

We > me.

Leadership shouldn't be about how we can get more people to follow us but about how we can empower those already following us to be great leaders. How can we take the information from this book and help our coworkers and neighbors and siblings by teaching them how to succeed as Competitors? How can we invest in such people by helping them learn to compete, every day, for their lives?

If we cling to the philosophy of building only our following, then we lose the opportunity to create more leaders—and, in turn, to create bigger impacts. Think about how a coaching tree works.

A great NFL coach teaches the team's assistants his philosophies, his strategies, and his leadership skills. The more successful the coach is, the more knowledge and experience he'll have to pass on to his younger coaches. Eventually those coaches leave for head-coaching jobs, bringing with them all of the knowledge and influence from their mentor. The original coach is able to teach and to empower his assistants, and once they leave, that influence continues on with them.

Hall of Fame football coach Bill Walsh, the architect of the NFL's "west coast offense," has a coaching tree a mile high.[39] Elements of his offensive strategy (which changed the game when it debuted) can be seen in today's game, as coaches Andy Reid (Kansas City), Jon Gruden (Oakland), Sean McVay (Los Angeles), and others came from Walsh's tree after passing through former Green Bay and Seattle coach Mike Holmgren. Even if they never worked directly with Walsh, many coaches and teams today are influenced by his leadership.

When we focus solely on building a following, our impact is limited to the first degree—only on those we directly interact with. Once we retire or die, that following starts to shrink, because it's solely determined by those we directly touch.

When we focus on empowering other leaders, our impact is limitless. The leaders with whom we directly interact and whom we empower will, in turn, interact with and empower others, advancing our impact to a second degree. That group will do the same for another, and we grow our reach and influence to a third degree, a fourth degree, a fifth degree, and beyond. We create a "coaching tree" of Competitors. We impact each person (at work, at church, at home) because of how we empowered our first network.

A big following doesn't make you a great leader. How you invest in that following does.

Worth Remembering

It's easy to forget that on a daily basis, our legacy is created by our daily choices. Legacy is a big concept, which. if we're honest, is usually pushed to the side amidst the chaos of life's busy schedule.

I think if we created space and had an honest conversation, many of us would admit we've thought about our legacy. We wonder what others will say about us after we're gone. We wonder who will be there at the end, maybe what their last words to us will be, and, after we're gone, how they'll remember us.

Some of us may even fear that we won't be remembered at all.

Here's the thing: we may think right now that others will remember how much money we had, what position we held at work, or what great thing we said. In reality, our legacy is defined by only two things:

1. How we helped others

2. How we lived our lives

Good or bad, those two things create our lasting legacies. This truth should challenge you to stop worrying about what you say as much how you live. It should encourage you to stop worrying about having the right pictures to post online, the right number of "0s" in your bank account to be considered success-ful; instead, it should challenge you to focus on what choices you make each day.

I've never been to a retirement party where toasts men-tioned how much money the retiree made or how nice her office was. I have yet to attend a funeral where ministers read off the deceased's bank statements or social media following.

I have heard about how this one employee was always mento-ring the new hires to make sure they were set up for success. I've heard friends rave about a dead person's kindness in always mak-ing time to have a cup of coffee and deep conversation. I've been inspired by hearing stories of how someone dead lived his or her life to the fullest, seizing each day for all it had and refusing to simply float through life.

I've heard time and time again how they helped others and what kind of life they lived, because in the end that's what mat-ters most.

The choices that we make with our limited time here and what actions we take during our life paint the biggest pieces of our legacy. Winning our work, our workouts, and our lives isn't about the stock options we cash in, the weights we lift, or the headlines that we receive. Winning those things is about the lives we impact in the process, the example that we set with our actions, and the choices that we make to be better than we were yesterday, every day.

What you're remembered for will never show up in your bank account or in your follower count. What you're remembered for is the impact you leave behind on others and the actions you take to inspire those that are still here.

Help Others Win, Too

Our legacies as leaders will be defined by the ones that we helped learn to lead.

Career

1. Invest time to help all new hires get "up to speed" on the company, the culture, and the keys to success in their roles. Be a resource for helping them to succeed. Be the person you wish you had met when you started working there.

2. Make time for the ones who want to learn from you. Don't open your calendar up to everyone, and protect your time aggressively, but find opportunities to support and teach the ambitious who want to learn how they can also succeed. Give them questions to answer and actions to complete. If they don't answer the questions or complete the actions, stop investing your time. If they do, keep pouring into them as they continue to grow.

Health and Fitness

1. You are more than the number on a scale. Remember: our goal should be to live a long and healthy life. Don't get frustrated if you don't lift as much as someone else or if you lack their six-pack abs. Maintain focus on competing against yourself every day and improving.

2. Share your story. Don't just post the perfections online. Be authentic. Share your struggles. Encourage those who may

be starting down the same path that you were on years ago, and encourage those on that same journey now.

Personal Life

1. Be a mentor. Invest time each month to help someone succeed professionally or personally. There are limitless opportunities within organizations and nonprofit groups, like Big Brothers Big Sisters, to help someone younger than you succeed.

2. If you've had success in a certain endeavor, don't be afraid to help teach others how you did it. Don't be tricked into believing success is limited—there are enough wins out there to share with more people. Be the light that shines the way for them.

Chapter Takeaways

1. Leadership isn't about how many followers we can accumulate online or offline. It's about how many other leaders we can help create and empower.

2. Competitors are focused on how they can invest in helping their networks succeed, instead of how many followers they can accumulate.

3. Our legacy is created by how we help others and how we live our lives. Let your actions leave no doubt about the type of Competitor—and person—you are.

10

Ending on Empty

Compete with everything you've got.

I remember my mom telling me to only worry about doing my best before a test or sports game. She didn't care about the outcome, only that I did the very best I could in that moment. I imagine you've heard something similar from a parent, a coworker, or a friend. I've encouraged friends to do their best before an interview or a big presentation.

I know they have the ability to excel within them, but more than that, I want them to be the type of person who goes all-out in that moment, instead of risking a specific feeling most of us know too well.

A feeling of *regret.*

Have you ever felt regret after a game for not playing your best?

Have you ever left an interview kicking yourself for not being more prepared?

Have you ever felt as though you didn't give your best effort in preparation or performance and that it caused you to come up short at some point along the way?

Regret is a common feeling for most people you know. This isn't the same type of feeling you have when another player or team is just flat-out better and when, despite your best performance, you still come up short.

Every athlete walks off the field of a competition in only one of two ways.

He may walk off with regret, knowing that somewhere in the practice and preparation of the off-season or week leading up to the game, he dropped the ball. Maybe he took workouts off; maybe he wasn't as locked in during film sessions; or maybe he drank copious amounts of alcohol and neglected the nutrition plan.

Perhaps it was none of that; instead, he simply took plays off during the game, believing in the moment that one play here or there wasn't that big of a deal—but after the game, he walks off the field, wondering how much those plays could've changed the game. He knows that he didn't do his best to prepare, to practice, or to play in this game, and he wonders *what if* he had?

Or an athlete may walk off the field with her head held high. She knows she did her absolute best in every practice. She studied films religiously. She played her heart out during the game. She walks off the field, regardless of what the scoreboard reads, confident that she gave everything that she had in the pursuit of every goal that the team set. She doesn't ask herself 'what if,' because she knows that she did everything in her power to give herself an opportunity to win.

Some days you just have "it," while other days are a struggle. In a physical sense, you may walk into the gym today, and the weights seem light. You fly through the workout and feel as if you could keep this pace up all day long. Tomorrow may be a different story. That same weight may feel a ton heavier, and you might struggle to make it even through a twenty-minute workout.

Your best may vary. Some days, you're sick, tired, or worn down. Other days, you're filled with energy and life. In each day—in each *moment*—Competitors will give the best of what they've got. Competitors leave every opportunity, knowing that they did everything that they could in that moment.

Compare that with the feeling of regret.

The Two Scariest Words

Regret leaves you with the two scariest words in the human language: "what if." We ask ourselves those two words when we know we failed to show up in the moment as our best self, moments when

- Instead of approaching that attractive coworker we've been wanting to ask out, we avoid her, only to soon find out we missed our window and will never get the chance now that she's met someone else.

- We spend Thursday night out drinking with friends, then show up hungover to give a presentation Friday morning, and we end up bombing it.

- We put off finally going on that trip—you know, the one we've talked about going on every year—for just another year, when "timing is better." Eventually, we put it off long enough that we never go, and one day we look back with regret, asking ourselves "what if" we'd just gone the first time that we wanted to.

"What if" questions can haunt us our entire lives, because we know that we left something on the table, that we had more within us in that moment, and that we chose not to act.

More in the Tank

My brain has told me on more than one occasion that I was about to die if I didn't stop moving. Usually, it's screaming during a brutal workout or a long run that death is imminent. It's pleading with me to slow down, usually creating a storm of inner dialogue about wanting to fend off death versus pushing through the pain.

As you can tell by reading this book, I didn't die. Even on the days that my brain swore that I was about to.

I may have rolled around on the ground, fighting off the lactic-acid pain and struggling to get air in my lungs, but eventually I returned to normal. Like most of you who are nodding along, recalling a terrible workout, I returned to the gym within a day or two.

I didn't die as I thought I was going to. I finished the workout. I even went back for more.

How many of us during our sports career thought we had nothing left in the tank, only to realize that the game was almost over? We suddenly felt a rush of energy and strength that we didn't realize that we had, and we focused on the importance of the next deciding play.

Our brains will trick us into believing that we're tapped out, we're exhausted, we're completely spent, and that if we continue, we'll die. But somehow, we find the reserves to keep going, and if we can keep going, it means we aren't empty yet. Right?

When your "Fuel Low" light turns on in your car, you may panic that you're out of gas. In reality, your car can probably keep running another twenty to thirty miles. The gauge may say empty, but your car still has a little gasoline left. It'll run until it runs out, and finally stops dead.

The light in our brains may come on, warning us that we're out of fuel, but in reality, we still have some left in the tank. Most of us just give up when that warning light comes on. Competitors keep pushing, determined to exhaust themselves until there's truly nothing left.

If they don't, they know they've quit with something still left inside to give.

We question "what if" when we stop running our hardest because that voice says we're about to die, and then we miss hitting a PR by two seconds.

We look back and ask "what if," when we let fear talk us out of showing up as our best for that interview, because we're afraid we're not ready for that level yet.

Then one day, we look up and realize that we're out of time. We missed our opportunity and still had more energy in the tank. We kick ourselves, because we gave in when that small voice inside told us we didn't have what it took to succeed, instead of pushing ourselves until our tank was truly empty.

Just as athletes can walk off the field knowing that they gave their all in practice, preparation, and performance and are satisfied because they know that they did everything that they could with everything that they had, wouldn't it be great to end our careers in that same way?

Wouldn't it be great to end our *lives* that way?

No asking "what if."

No cheating ourselves of an opportunity by giving less than our best.

No leaving any hopes, dreams, or energy in the tank.

Competitors end on empty.

What's More Important

One of the things that I love most about sports is how they prove that a great finish can overcome a slow start. A bad half is frequently overcome by teams willing to compete in every play, even if they're behind on the scoreboard.

Imagine being down 28–3 at the half-time of a playoff football game to a team that just one week before had beaten you 27–3 to end the regular season. Your starting quarterback has been out, and your backup has struggled to get the offense going. You realize that if you're going to win this game, it's going to take every player making every play the entire second half. You're not even sure if that's going to be enough.

Then your backup quarterback starts the second half by throwing an interception that's returned for a touchdown. The scoreboard now reads 35–3. You don't even look into the stands, because you already know that your fans are starting to leave, quitting on the game and the season with twenty-eight minutes left to play. Honestly, you can't even blame them. *No one comes back from that big of a deficit.*

Your opponent is already thinking about its next game, while you can't help fighting off thoughts of your impending off-season start. You're down a starting quarterback. Other players are hurt. Somehow you've got to rally and score thirty-two unanswered points with backups at two of your most important positions.

All hope seems lost. The odds are against you. Every bounce of the ball seems to go the wrong way. Have you ever felt that way? One thing after another, after another, and you just can't seem to catch a break.

We try to pay off our debt, but every move we take forward seems to further put us behind, and we watch as our bills and debt continues to mount.

We lose a job because of downsizing only a month after we left our previous company for this new role.

We spend a few years getting our health back to the peak shape we had in our teens, only to get a terrible diagnosis from our doctor.

We find ourselves at rock bottom, unsure if we can crawl our way out. To be honest, most people don't.

A Competitor will use that rock bottom as a stepping-stone to move forward.

That football team losing 35–3 could have very easily quit on the season right there. What happened next will go down in NFL history.

Remember backup quarterback Frank Reich that I mentioned earlier in the book? He led a thirty-eight-point rally, helping the Buffalo Bills win the biggest comeback in NFL history, a 41–38 overtime win against the Houston Oilers.

No matter how the first quarter—or first three quarters—of our life has started, the final one is where the magic happens. If we're still breathing, that final quarter isn't over yet. We determine the outcome by how we choose to compete, *starting right now.*

Each one of us has the opportunity to *choose* to be a Competitor.

It's a choice that we get to make each morning, because it's not about anyone else. It's only about ourselves and whom we see looking back in the mirror at us. Will today be a day that I choose to show up and...

- Outwork my talent

- Not let a hard day break me

- Embrace my process to get better

- Choose my teammates for life

- Lead with my actions

- Do my best, no matter how I feel

- Help others win, too

- End it on empty

Will today be the day that I choose to do these things or not? It's a choice and not an easy one, but it becomes easier when you adopt the mindset to compete for your life every day.

It's about choosing to be a winning Competitor to excel in your career, to overcome any obstacles that you encounter in life, and to step into being the person you were created to be.

Then help others to do the same.

The world needs more Competitors in it, and I hope today is the day you join the ranks.

Yours in competition,

Jake

(In case you missed it)

You are invited to join the Compete Every Day community.

You are invited to join the thousands of ambitious Competitors claiming victory in their professional and personal lives in our free Facebook community at:

www.Facebook.com/groups/CompeteEveryDay

Inside this community, you will find thousands of driven leaders just like you who are making strong choices to compete every day in their work, workouts, and life.

I am excited to meet you, encourage you, and hold you accountable to achieving the important goals you've set for your career and life.

APPENDIX AND RESOURCES

02: Why Competition Matters–page 14, Citations page 35

[1] Jeremy P. Jamieson, Wendy Berry Mendez, and Matthew K. Nock. "Improving Acute Stress Responses: The Power of Reappraisal." *APS Psychological* Science. Rochester, NY: 2012.

[2] Bronson, Po, & Merryman, Ashley (2014). *Top Dog: The Science of Winning & Losing.* Twelve Publishing

[3] Bronnie Ware. *The Top Five Regrets of the Dying: A Life Transported by the Dearly Departed* (blog).

[4] Jennings, John. (2018, January 18) "How Many People Finish Books?" *The IFOD.* https://www.theifod.com/how-many-people-finish-books/

03: Outwork Your Talent–page 35, Citations page 54

[5] *Draft Express*, 2006. See URL: http://www.draftexpress.com/article/Jose-Juan-Barea-NBA-Draft-Scouting-Report-2788/

[6] *Basketball Reference.* 2006 NBA Draft. See URL: https://www.basketball-reference.com/draft/NBA_2006.html

[7] Malcolm Gladwell. (2016, May 13). *What makes a great competitor (Quarterback)* [Video]. YouTube. https://youtu.be/bM1ECS72GWE

[8] *NFL Full Draft History.* NFL.com (http://www.nfl.com/draft/history/fulldraft?type=team)

[9] ESPN. Jake Trotter. "Annoying Little Brother Baker Mayfield Once Aspired to Be Like His Browns Backup." See URL: https://www.espn.com/nfl/story/_/id/27399903/annoying-little-brother-baker-mayfield-once-aspired-his-browns-backup

[10] Angela Duckworth. *Grit: The Power of Passion and Perseverance*. New York: Scribner, 2016

[11] Rick Brewer. "Michael Jordan—The College Days." See URL: https://goheels.com/news/1999/6/21/205488075.aspx

[12] Dweck, Carol. *Mindset: The New Psychology of Success*. New York: Random House, 2006.

[13] Zak Keefer. "The Best Peyton Manning Stories You've Ever Heard." *rIndy Star*. October 4, 2017. See URL: https://www.indystar.com/story/sports/nfl/colts/2017/10/04/peyton-manning-best-stories-youve-never-heard/731585001/

[14] Tony Robbins Interview. See URL: https://www.youtube.com/watch?v=-XdUjc-InxE&t=924s

[15] ESPN Stats Twitter: https://twitter.com/ESPNStatsInfo/status/992973492231524352

04: Never Let the Hard Days Win–page 55, Citations page 74

[16] Ravn, Karen (2013, February 16). "Bet you can't read this as fast as your friend can." *Los Angeles Times*, https://www.latimes.com/health/la-xpm-2013-feb-16-la-he-top-dog-20130216-story.html

[17] *Impact Theory*. (2018, February 16). "Quitting" | Nastia Liukin on Impact Theory Facebook. https://www.facebook.com/watch/?v=1623724771074479

[18] *30 for 30*, *Bad Boys*, ESPN, Vol. II, no. 18

[19] "Single Season Leaders for Batting Average." https://www.baseball-almanac.com/hitting/hibavg2.shtml

05: Embrace the Process–page 75, Citations page 106

[20] *National Geographic*. (2005). "Flash facts about lightning." https://www.nationalgeographic.com/news/2005/6/flash-facts-about-lightning/

[21] *The Joe Rogan Experience*. (2010, October 29). Episode 1278 – Kevin Hart. http://podcasts.joerogan.net/podcasts/kevin-hart

[22] *Science First*. "10 Interesting Facts About the Human Brain." https://www.sciencefirst.com/10-interesting-facts-about-the-human-brain/

[23] Ryback, Ralph M.D. (2016). "The Science of Accomplishing Your Goals." *Psychology Today*. https://www.psychologytoday.com/us/blog/the-truisms-wellness/201610/the-science-accomplishing-your-goals

[24] Khalil, Shireen. (2018, December 31). "Most people give up New Year's Resolutions by January 12, study claims." *Fox News*. https://www.foxnews.com/lifestyle/most-people-give-up-new-years-resolutions-by-january-12-study-claims

[25] Dotson, Charles O., Iso-Ahola, Seppo E. (2016)." Psychological Momentum – A Key to Continued Success." *Frontiers in Psychology*, Front Psychol. 2016; 7: 1328. Published online 2016 Aug 31. doi: 10.3389/fpsyg.2016.01328 PMCID: PMC5006010

06: Build Your Starting Lineup–page 107, Citations page 126

[26] SuperMoneyHustler. (2011, August 15). *Jim Rohn 5 – The Law of Averages* [Video]. YouTube. https://youtu.be/IPYzLfWuyoI

[27] Roosevelt, Theodore.. (1910). "Citizenship in a Republic" [Speech].

[28] Restrepo, Sandra. (Director). (2019). *The Call to Courage* [Film]. Netflix.

[29] Savage, Phil. (2017). *4th and Goal Every Day: Alabama's Relentless Pursuit of Perfection*. St. Martin's Press.

[30] Air Jordan. (2012, February 16). *Michael Jordan—Failure*. YouTube. https://youtu.be/GuXZFQKKF7A

[31] Wong, Y. Joel. (2014). *The Psychology of Encouragement: Theory, Research, and Applications*. The Counseling Psychologist. 2014; doi: 10.1177/0011000001454509I

[32] Streep, Peg. (2013, August 20). "Why Words Can Hurt at Least as Much as Sticks and Stones." *Psychology Today*. https://www.psychologytoday.com/us/blog/tech-support/201308/ why-words-can-hurt-least-much-sticks-and-stones

07: Lead with Your Actions–page 128, Citations page 142

[33] Harris, John. (2017, February 22). "Moses Fleetwood Walker was the first African American to play pro baseball, six decades before Jackie Robinson." *The Undefeated*. https://theundefeated.com/features/moses-fleetwood-walker-was-the-first-african-american-to-play-pro-baseball-six-decades-before-jackie-robinson/

[34] *Wikipedia*. (2020). "Jackie Robinson." https://en.wikipedia.org/wiki/ Jackie_Robinson

[35] "Career Leaders for Batting Average." https://www.baseball-almanac.com/ hitting/hibavg1.shtml

08: Always Do Your Best–page 143, Citations page 160

[36] Long, Mark. (2019, March 11). "Nick Foles to sign 4-year, $88 million contract with the Jacksonville Jaguars." *Business Insider*. https://www.businessinsider.com/ ap-source-foles-to-sign-4-year-88m-deal-with-jaguars-2019-3

[37] Keefer, Zach. (2018, February 16). "The backup, the pastor, the coach: Frank Reich's road to the Colts." IndyStar. https://www.indystar.com/story/sports/ nfl/colts/2018/02/16/backup-pastor-coach-frank-reichs-road-colts/344105002/

[38] Evon, Dan. (2019, January 25). "Did Jim Thorpe Wear Mismatched Shoes at the 1912 Olympics?" *Snopes.com*. https://www.snopes.com/fact-check/ jim-thorpe-shoes-olympics/

09: Help Others Win, Too–page 161, Citations page 166

[39] Kilgore, Adam. (2018, October 12) "Branching out." *The Washington Post*. https://www.washingtonpost.com/graphics/2018/sports/ nfl-coaching-trees-connecting-every-active-coach/